D1162489

A Legal Perspective for
Student Personnel Administrators

A Legal Perspective
for
Student Personnel
Administrators

By

ROBERT LAUDICINA, Ph.D.

Dean of Students
Fairleigh Dickinson University
Madison, New Jersey

and

JOSEPH L. TRAMUTOLA, JR., J.D.

Associate Professor of Business
Fairleigh Dickinson University
Madison, New Jersey

CHARLES C THOMAS · PUBLISHER
Springfield · Illinois · U.S.A.

Published and Distributed Throughout the World by
CHARLES C THOMAS • PUBLISHER
Bannerstone House
301-327 East Lawrence Avenue, Springfield, Illinois, U.S.A.

© *1974, by* CHARLES C THOMAS • PUBLISHER
ISBN 0-398-03080-4
Library of Congress Catalog Card Number: 73-20356

With THOMAS BOOKS careful attention is given to all details of manufacturing and design. It is the Publisher's desire to present books that are satisfactory as to their physical qualities and artistic possibilities and appropriate for their particular use. THOMAS BOOKS will be true to those laws of quality that assure a good name and good will.

Printed in the United States of America
C-1

Library of Congress Cataloging in Publication Data
Laudicina, Robert.
    A legal perspective for student personnel administrators.
      1. Students—Legal status, laws, etc.—United
States. 2. Universities and colleges—Law and
legislation—United States. I. Tramutola, Joseph,
joint author. II. Title.
KF4243.L38   344'.73'079   73-20356
ISBN 0-398-03080-4

For
Eleanor
and
Mary Ann

Preface

WITH THE REDUCTION of the age of majority from twenty-one to eighteen years in almost half of the states, college administrators must be fully aware that there has been a radical shift in the relationship between college and student. Certain conventional administrative practices may no longer be viable, given the new adulthood of students. College administrators, indeed, must be sensitive to and aware of the legal implications and consequences of decisions that they make every day. It is the purpose of this book to help student personnel administrators analyze situations, utilizing both educational and legal perspectives.

It is an American tradition that great controversies of fact and opinion ultimately reach the courts. And so, campus unrest in the sixties heightened the legal awareness of students and other members of the campus community. As students and their colleges came to the courtroom door, administrative discretion yielded to judicial interpretation. We have attempted, therefore, to develop an administrative framework wherein student personnel administrators can determine whether proper judgment and execution of university policy has been made. With courts increasingly asked to review educationally based controversies, college administrators must be able to plan and articulate college policy so that frequent legal confrontation can be avoided.

Chapter I introduces a series of important questions for the student personnel administrator—questions which have both legal and educational implications. Chapter II reviews traditional legal theory in light of changing student and institutional relationships. Chapter III examines the student's civic and campus responsibilities. This chapter notes the difference in due process requirements for public and private institutions.

Chapter IV analyzes student drug abuse *vis-a-vis* relevant case materials and federal laws. Chapter V reviews the rights of students in the light of recent judicial decisions and provides model university and campus policies.

Chapter VI notes what we consider to be the most appropriate educational framework for administrative decision-making. Chapter VII notes several categories of student-related issues and problems which college administrators should carefully examine.

It is our intention that this book serve as a set of unique guidelines so that college administrators may more successfully deal with day by day situations. Such guidelines should tend to prevent crisis decision-making.

We hope that this book will become a valuable resource for all those who work with or who are interested in the student's relationship with his educational institution. Readers should recognize that this book neither replaces competent legal counsel nor creates a fixed set of administrative practices.

ROBERT LAUDICINA
JOSEPH L. TRAMUTOLA, JR.
Fairleigh Dickinson University

Contents

A Legal Perspective for
Student Personnel Administrators

CHAPTER I

A Legal Perspective for Student Personnel Administrators

PERHAPS ONE OF MOST important concerns of the student personnel administrator today is the law, and yet nowhere in his graduate training or in his preparation for administrative work is the law carefully studied. Occasionally, the student personnel administrator may attend training sessions which deal with the law, but rarely is any systematic, educative method pursued in sensitizing the student personnel administrator to the legal implications and consequences of decisions he may make.

Law is a result of social custom and institutionalization of norms. Indeed, we live in a society governed by laws, and those laws must be administered by men. The law is an effective instrument for use within the university, but it must be implemented with restraint and even reluctance. The law, moreover, cannot be used by the administrator to avoid the difficult task of decision-making. It is the function of the administrator to analyze situations utilizing his own training and educational perspective along with the expertise of a lawyer. However, it is not the role of lawyers to make decisions for the educational administrator.

The administrator must assure that a sensible educational judgment has been made before resorting to the fundamentally impersonal rules which make up the stuff of the law. The law, then, cannot be and should not be used as a simple avenue for providing answers to educational and administrative problems. Nevertheless, the complexity of administrative decision-making today requires a working relationship with legal counsel. Such a relationship, although not precluding the use of conventionally retained university attorneys, requires periodic, regular and personal meetings between student personnel administrator and legal counsel, knowledgeable and empathetic to those problems most commonly arising in the university community.

3

Until recently, student personnel administrators were surrogate parents and their decisions regarding a student's personal and academic growth were rarely questioned. Parietal rules, rules requiring class attendance, and rules which forbade alcoholic beverages were subject only to existing social values as interpreted by the individual student personnel administrator. Massive social change in the 1960's, as reflected in liberated Supreme Court statements, has heightened the legal awareness of students and other members of the campus community, altering the form and content of the *in loco parentis* concept. The locus of power within the academic community has thereby shifted from individual administrators who formerly were able to unilaterally make policy to tripartite groups made up of students, faculty and administrators.

This democratized colleague approach now compels student personnel administrators to adjust their role, and to emphasize communitization of all campus constituencies. The student personnel administrator, then, should attempt to develop a framework of administrative operation where campus citizens sit together, work together and decide together.

Student personnel administrators, in addition, should develop their role as a bridge between campus and civic constituencies. The creation and development of viable volunteer and cooperative education programs is for the student personnel administrator an important objective.

The student personnel administrator now faces many new questions, especially with regard to contractual relationships, the use of alcohol, drugs and controlled dangerous substances on campus, and the protection of students' civil rights. One of the purposes of this book is to examine the law, not only as it affects students, but also as it affects the student personnel administrator and his function within the educational arena.

Law is an aspect of social organization. Law, in the Weberian sense, excludes informal social controls, and embraces only that phase of formal control dealing directly with rule enforcement. The more complex a social organization, the more likely the need for formal controls. Law, then, is the formal means of social control that involves the use of rules that are interpreted and are enforceable by the courts of a political community.[1] Under our system of law, the rights and duties of individuals are known beforehand, and the discretion of authorities in individual cases is limited either by judicial decisions or statutes, oftentimes with constitutional implications. Lawyers, who are specialists in the law, must determine whether a course of action has violated the law or is liable to do so in the future.

Education by its very nature deals with uncertainty and change. It deals with what we are and what we wish to become. Education is essentially a process of assessment and evaluation. It is particularly interested in the sources and consequences of problems. The law is more oriented to questions of *whether* something has occurred; education is more oriented to *why* something has happened.

Professional educators study, and do have expertise in, the developmental process of an individual, that is, his personal and intellectual growth. Traditionally, educators in the United States have had much discretion in formulating rules regulating a student's academic and social development. Admission procedures, rules regarding personal behavior, curriculum prerequisites and graduation requirements are all examples of those areas in which the college administrator has exercised full authority.

Courts in the past were most often asked in judicial controversies to determine whether an institution had proper jurisdictional authority, leaving questions of discretion and judgement solely to the administrator. Racing technological and social changes, particularly since World War II, have altered traditional relationships between individuals and institutions. Because of such changes, courts in recent years have tended to examine the relationships between individuals and institutions, and have been more likely to determine whether proper judgement and execution of university policy has been made by a campus administrator. No longer does the judiciary avoid controversies related to college housing, educational opportunities, rights of enfranchisement, dis-

---

1. F. J. Davis, *Society and the Law* (Glencoe, Free Press, 1962) , p. 41.

cipline and sanctions and the guarantee of procedural due process. Can a private university, for example, tow away cars parked in areas reserved for faculty with judicial impunity? Can a resident student's contract be terminated because he has cooking appliances in his room, or if his girlfriend sleeps over on a weekend? Can a dean suspend a student after he has received three signed letters from students indicating that another student is selling narcotics on campus?

The past highly discretionary role of a dean of students, consequently, has been sharply limited by both the decisions of the courts and also a heightened legal sensitivity of the student body. The due process clauses of the Fifth and Fourteenth Amendments have been and will become in the future the touchstone for restricting the dean's discretionary authority. Legal implications of the dean's new consultative role are portentious in that they involve questions related to whether a student has received due process and whether an institution's regulations are reasonable. In addition, the educational implications of those questions relate to a student's personal growth and the kind of mind-to-mind contact that is likely to take place between student and educational administrator.

CHAPTER II

A Historical Note

ALTHOUGH THE LAW is an effective and fair instrument for use within the university, our present concern should be with the problem of how and where one uses the law effectively. Traditional legal theories as applied to students and the institutions they attend must now be examined in light of changing legal and social patterns.

The concept that a college stands *in loco parentis,* and as such has the power to control the personal conduct and academic growth of a student much as a parent might, has been generally abandoned. However, it should be noted that students may at times selectively seek a return to the *in loco parentis* concept where it is of special advantage to them, i.e. students may ask that police not come to campus and arrest those persons using drugs, but that such use remain an intramural matter for campus administrative determination.

In actual fact, the doctrine of *in loco parentis* was a convenient fiction utilized to buttress the sometimes questionable authority of college officialdom. It no longer serves this function because of the increased role of the university with regard to its service to the community and the demands of students to participate in all phases of decision-making, both in the civic and campus communities. The classical concept of the university, separate in all of its phases from the community, simply no longer exists. Along the same lines, the concept that a university has inherent authority to make all rules and regulations affecting the student life of its campus, and that the student is, therefore, subject to those rules is now a disregarded myth. Today's reality is that the rules of the community within which the university lives have priority. No longer, for example, can college administrators develop effective rules separate from those that have been formulated by civic officials. Campus regulations relating to parking,

7

residence, guests and visitors to the campus, and the right to carry firearms are now subject to judicial consideration. A recent New Jersey lower court decision, for example, reversed a campus penalty against a student who had parked his automobile in a proscribed area because of improper notice.

Another basis for administrative authority is predicated upon a contractual relationship, that is, the school agrees to furnish education and services for which the student pays. Conversely, the student agrees to abide by campus regulations. The contract theory has certain latitude and can be a good basis for examining the rights of a student vis à vis the university. An important source of student contractual rights and obligations may be found in institutional bulletins and catalogues. With an increasing number of states lowering the age of majority, the contractual theory of authority of the university is gaining greater usability.

There is renewed interest in the theory that the university is a fiduciary vis à vis the student, and this relationship can be used for establishing student rights. The fiduciary concept assumes that the university is a repository of administrative authority entrusted by its charter to formulate rules and manage resources for the benefit of the student body. Previously, this fiduciary concept was used to limit the rights of students by denying to them participation in the operation of campus administration. The very nature of a trust agreement, of course, does permit such a distorted interpretation. Enlightened administration, however, could well use the fiduciary agreement concept to promote and encourage mutuality and reciprocity within the campus community.

College administrators now should reconsider the contractual and fiduciary basis of institutional authority in light of changing social and legal reality. Given the demise of the *in loco parentis* fiction, and the realization that a student has a dual citizenship in both the campus and civic community, administrators should be encouraged to develop a *de communitatis* basis for university authority. The *de communitatis* approach takes into account not only the rights of the university and its obligations to students, but also the recognition of shared responsibilities for the growth and direction of the institution. This approach emphasizes collegial relationships with common areas of work and interests among students, administrators and faculty. While not eliminating the potential for intramural campus conflict, the *de communitatis* concept can minimize individual differences and focus more on the goals of the institution itself. It then becomes a sound basis for university governance, fully recognizing legal, social and economic changes which have occurred in our society.

RELEVANT CASE MATERIALS

In Loco Parentis

Gott v. Berea College, et al.
156 Ky. 376 (161 S. W. 204)
December 11, 1913

Opinion of the Court by Judge Nunn—Affirming.

The appellant, J. S. Gott, about the first of September, 1911, purchased and was constructing a restaurant in Berea, Kentucky, across the street from the premises of Berea College. A restaurant had been conducted in this same place for quite a long while by the party from whom Gott purchased. For many years it has been the practice of the governing authorities of Berea College to distribute among the students at the beginning of each scholastic year a pamphlet entitled "Students' Manual," containing the rules and regulations of the college for the government of the student body. Subsection three of this manual under the heading "Forbidden Places" enjoined the students from entering any "place of ill repute, liquor saloons, gambling houses, etc."

During the 1911 summer vacation, the faculty, pursuant to their usual practice of revising the rules, added another clause to this rule as to forbidden places, and the rule was announced to the student body at chapel exercises on the first day of the fall term which began September eleventh. The new rule is as follows:

(b) Eating houses and places of amusement in Berea, not controlled by the College, must not be entered by students on pain of immediate dismissal. The institution provides for the recreation of its students, and ample accommodation for meals and refreshment, and cannot permit outside parties to solicit student patronage for gain.

Appellant's restaurant was located and conducted mainly for the profits arising from student patronage. During the first few days after the publication of this rule, two or three students were expelled for its violation, so that the making of the rule and its enforcement had the effect of very materially injuring, if not absolutely ruining, appellant's business because the students were afraid to further patronize it.

On the twentieth day of September appellant instituted this action in equity, and procured a temporary restraining order and injunction against the enforcement of the rule above quoted, and charging that the college and its officers unlawfully and maliciously conspired to injure his business by adopting a rule forbidding students from entering eating houses. For this he claimed damages in the sum of $500. By amended petitions, he alleged that in pursuance of such conspiracy the college officers had uttered slanderous remarks concerning him, and his business, and increased his prayer for damages to $2,000. The slanderous remarks were alleged to have been spoken at chapel, and other public exercises to the student body as a reason for the rule, and were to the effect that appellant was a bootlegger, and upon more than one occasion had been charged and convicted of illegally selling whiskey. Berea College answered, and denied that any slanderous remarks had been made as to appellant, or that they had conspired maliciously, or otherwise, or that the rule adopted was either unlawful or unreasonable. In the second paragraph the college affirmatively set forth that it is a private (incorporated) institution of learning, supported wholly by private donations, and its endowment, and such fees as it collects from students or parents of students who desire to become affiliated with said institution, and abide by and conform to the rules and regulations provided by the governing body. A student upon entering said institution agrees upon pain of dismissal to conform to such rules and regulations as may from time to time be promulgated; that the institution aims to furnish an education to inexperienced country, mountain boys and girls of very little means at the lowest possible cost; that practically all of the students are from rural districts, and unused to the ways of even a village the size of Berea, and that they are of very limited means. It is further alleged that they have been compelled from time to time to pass rules tending to prevent students from wasting their time and money, and to keep them wholly occupied in study; that some of the rules prohibited the doing of things not in themselves wrong, or unlawful, but which the governing authorities have found, and believe detrimental to the best interest of the college and the student body. For these reasons the rule in question was adopted, but they say that at the time they had no knowledge that the plaintiff owned, or was about to acquire a restaurant, and that the rule was in no way directed at the plaintiff. Upon motion the restraining order was dissolved, but on account of allegations charging slanderous remarks, the lower court overruled demurrer to the petition. After filing of the answer, proof was heard, the case submitted and tried by the court with the result that the petition was dismissed, and Gott appeals to this court.

The larger question, and the one we are called here to pass upon, is whether the rule forbidding students entering eating houses was a reasonable one, and within the power of the college authorities to enact, and the further question whether, in that event, appellant Gott will be heard to complain. That the enforcement of the rule worked a great injury to Gott's restaurant business cannot well be denied, but unless he can show that the college authorities have been guilty of a breach of some legal duty which they owe to him, he has no cause of action against them for the injury. One has no right of action against a merchant for refusal to sell goods, nor will an action lie, unless such means are used as of themselves constitute a breach of legal duty, for inducing or causing persons not to trade, deal or contract with another, and it is a well-established principle that when a lawful act is performed in the proper manner, the party performing it is not liable for mere incidental consequences injuriously resulting from it to another. . . .

College authorities stand in loco parentis concerning the physical and moral welfare, and mental training of the pupils, and we are unable to see why to that end they may not make any rule or regulation for the government or betterment of their pupils that a parent could for the same purpose. Whether the rules or regulations are wise, or their aims worthy, is a matter left solely to the discretion of the authorities, or parents as the case may be, and in the exercise of that discretion the courts are not disposed to interfere, unless the rules and aims are unlawful, or against public policy. . . . The corporate charter of Berea College empowers the board of trustees to "make such by-laws as it may deem necessary to promote the interest of the institution, not in violation of any laws of the State or the United States." This reference to the college powers shows that its authorities have a large discretion, and they are similar to the charter and corporate rights under which colleges and such institutions are generally conducted. Having in mind such powers, the courts have without exception held to the rule. . . .

A college or university may prescribe requirements for admission and rules for the conduct of its students, and one who enters as a student impliedly agrees to conform to such rules of government.

The only limit upon this rule is as to institutions supported in whole or in part by appropriations from the public treasury. In such cases their rules are viewed somewhat more critically, but since this is a private institution it is unnecessary to notice further the distinction.

Of course this rule is not intended to, nor will it be permitted to, interfere with parental control of children in the home, unless the acts forbidden materially affect the conduct and discipline of the school.

There is nothing in the case to show that the college had any contract, business or other direct relations with the appellant. They owed him no special duty, and while he may have suffered an injury, yet he does not show that the college is a wrong-doer in a legal or any sense. Nor does he show that in enacting the rules they did it unlawfully, or that they exceeded their power, or that there was any conspiracy to do anything unlawful. Their right to enact the rule comes within their charter provision, and that it was a reasonable rule cannot be very well disputed. Assuming that there were no other outside eating houses in Berea, and that there never had been a disorderly one, or one in which intoxicating liquors had been sold, still it would not be an unreasonable rule forbidding students entering or patronizing appellant's establishment. In the first place the college offers an education to the poorest, and undertakes to offer them the means of a livelihood within the institution while they are pursuing their studies, and at the same time provides board and lodging for a nominal charge. Whatever profit was derived served to still further reduce expenses charged against the pupil. It stands to reason that when the plans of the institution are so prepared, and the support and maintenance of the students are so ordered, that there must be the fullest cooperation on the part of all the students, otherwise there will be disappointment if not failure in the project.

It is also a matter of common knowledge that one of the chief dreads of college authorities is the outbreak of an epidemic, against which they should take the utmost precaution. These precautions, however, may wholly fail if students carelessly or indiscriminately visit or patronize public or unsanitary eating houses. Too often those operating such places are ignorant of, or indifferent to, even the simplest sanitary requirements. As a safeguard against disease infection from this source there is sufficient reason for the promulgation of the rule complained of. But even if it might be conceded that the rule was an unreasonable one, still appellant Gott is in no position to complain. He was not a student, nor is it shown that he had any children as students in the college. The rule was directed to and intended to control only the student body. For the purposes of this case, the school, its officers and students are a legal entity, as much so as any family, and as a father may direct his children, those in charge of boarding schools are well within their rights and powers when they direct their students what to eat and where they must get it, where they may go and what forms of amusement are forbidden.

Considering the whole case, the judgment of the lower court is affirmed.

Contract Theory

Jones v. Vassar College
299 NYS 283
April 15, 1969

W. Vincent Grady, Justice

Student protests and demonstrations are prevalent in many colleges and universities today. The instant case presents a related facet of the student-college relationship.

Vassar College, for over one hundred years, has been an all-female institution. In January of this year, it received approximately eighty male exchange students from various colleges. On March 5, a code of regulations and enforcement was passed unanimously by the student senate established under the terms of the new constitution of the Vassar College Student Government Association. It had been given the responsibility for enacting and enforcing undergraduate social regulations. These new rules and regulations changed the college's parietal regulations to permit the female students living in each corridor of the residential halls to decide whether or not they wished limitations to be placed upon the hours during which they might receive male guests in their rooms. An election was held on the proposed change, and 1,453 students voted. One thousand three hundred and seventy-five voted for "no restrictions" on visiting hours and sixty-eight students voted for a "limitation" on visiting hours without moving from their corridor. Ten students voted in favor of living in a corridor with "limited visiting hours," even if they would be required to move to a different corridor. It appears that the wishes of these ten students have been followed.

The president of Vassar College did not exercise his power of veto over the student-enacted legislation, thereby giving approval to the change in rules and regulations voted upon by the students and enacted by the Vassar College Student Government Association.

Plaintiff, Edna W. Jones, the mother of a Vassar College female student and on behalf of all parents of Vassar College students "similarly affected," commenced this action for a declaratory judgment that Vassar owed a duty to the plaintiffs to continue the former rules and regulations as pertains to parietals and for an injunction restraining the defendants from changing such rules and regulations. Plaintiffs herein seek an order to show cause, a temporary injunction and stay, although they demand the relief prayed for in the complaint. Thereafter, defendants moved for summary judgment, and this application is now before the court.

Plaintiffs' motion for "an order granting the relief prayed for in the . . . summons and verified complaint" is treated as a cross-motion for summary judgment.

There are three basic issues involved in this controversy:

1. Does Vassar College owe a legal obligation to the plaintiffs not to change its rules and regulations pertaining to social conduct on the college campus?

2. Have plaintiffs shown that there are issues of fact with regard to irreparable damage to their legal interests which require a trial on the merits?

3. Are there any issues of fact with respect to whether a declaratory judgment should be granted?

A review of the case law involving the student-college relationship does not reveal any case dealing with the issue as to whether a college has a contractual obligation not to change its rules and regulations governing social conduct.

Plaintiffs herein claim that there was an abuse of discretion on the part of Vassar College in permitting its students to make new rules and regulations with no restrictions on the visiting hours of males. Plaintiffs allege that this was a drastic change which constituted a breach of contract entitling the plaintiffs to the relief sought.

There is no genuine dispute as to any of the material facts surrounding the adoption and application of the new rules and regulations and the defendants concede that such change is drastic. However, does a drastic change in social rules and regulations, by a college, constitute a breach of its implied contract with a student or her parents? It is not controverted that all of the rules and regulations of Vassar, whether disciplinary, social or academic, are subject to constant review. The Bulletin of Vassar College, Student Handbook Issue 1968-1969, states with respect to such regulations:

> These regulations have been kept to the minimum deemed necessary to secure and maintain decent and orderly conditions of living and working for all the members of this residential college. Within this basic framework, the individual student shall be as free as possible to conduct her own academic and nonacademic life. This assumes that individual decisions will be accompanied by careful consideration of the standards maintained by the group. The privilege of making independent decisions involves the acceptance of a penalty should such choices violate either the spirit or the letter of the regulations (p. 31).

The Vassar Catalogue for 1968-1969 also states that the "College expects students to uphold its standards of personal and social conduct at all times when they are associated with Vassar" (p. 193).

The position of the plaintiffs is that the above statements in the Bulletin and Catalogue of Vassar College do not permit the college to change its rules and regulations as it has done herein.

As the court so aptly stated in Sweezy v. State of New Hampshire:

> The essentiality of freedom in the community of American universities is almost self-evident. No one should underestimate the vital role in a democracy that is played by those who guide and train our youth. To impose any straitjacket upon the intellectual leaders in our colleges and universities would imperil the future of our Nation. No field of education is so thoroughly comprehended by man that new discoveries cannot yet be made. Particularly is that true in the social sciences, where few, if any, principles are accepted as absolutes. Scholarship cannot flourish in an atmosphere of suspicion and distrust. Teachers and students must always remain free to inquire, to study and to evaluate, to gain new maturity and understanding; otherwise our civilization will stagnate and die.

(1) In academic communities greater freedoms may prevail than in society at large and the subtle fixing of these limits should, to a great degree, be left to the educational institution itself (Goldberg v. Regents of University of California, 248 Cal. App.2d 867, 57 Cal. Rptr. 463). The judiciary must exercise restraint in questioning the wisdom of specific rules or the manner of their application, since such matters are ordinarily in the prerogative of school administrators rather than the courts (Barker v. Hardway, D. C., 283 F. Supp. 228).

(2) There has been no showing by plaintiffs that there was an abuse of discretion by defendants in approving and adopting the new rules and regulations and this court will not interfere with defendant's discretion.

(3, 4) The plaintiffs urge that the court should interfere to protect alleged invasions of the students' right of privacy by forbidding unlimited visiting hours for males; however, as a matter of law, the plaintiffs are not entitled to an injunction since the complaint and other affidavits do not show that the plaintiffs have suffered or will suffer immediate and irreparable damage. Mere speculation as to the possible consequences of conduct complained of in the complaint is insufficient ...

(5, 6) The plaintiffs also seek a declaratory judgment, but the court cannot substitute its judgment as to the propriety of the new rules and regulations governing visiting hours of males for that of the administrative body which formulates such rules and regulations. Plaintiffs have failed to show a breach of the implied contract with the student or parent causing the plaintiffs irreparable injury; therefore, there are no legal rights of the plaintiffs which have been violated and declaratory judgment does not lie.

(7) Private colleges and universities are governed on the principle of academic self-regulation, free from judicial restraints (See Developments in the Law—Academic Freedom, 81 Harv. L. Rev. 1045). Vassar College, like other previously all-female institutions, has succumbed to the trend of coeducation, and with the advent of males, new difficulties will be encountered by the college administration. It is the privilege of a college, through its Student Government Association, to promulgate and enforce rules and regulations for the social conduct of students without judicial interference.

Defendants' motion for summary judgment is granted and the relief requested by plaintiffs is denied in all respects.

Fiduciary Theory

Bogust, et al. v. Iverson
10 Wis. 2d 129 (102 N. W. 2d 228)
April 5, 1960

Martin, Chief Justice

Defendant is "an educator by profession." Jeannie Bogust was born May 3, 1939. At the times referred to in the complaint she was a pupil at Stout State College where defendant was employed as a full-time director of student personnel services and professor of education with a Ph.D. degree. It is alleged that in such capacity the defendant was "charged with the maintenance of a counseling and testing center for personal, vocational, educational, scholastic or other problems, including those students torn by conflicting feelings which cause worry and social ineffectiveness."

The complaint states that commencing in November, 1957, Jeannie, as a student of the college, was under the direct guidance and supervision of the defendant; that defendant administered to her aptitude and personality tests and he was familiar with her personal, social and educational problems and her conflicting feeling, environment and social ineffectiveness; that he was well aware of her emotional disturbances, social conflicts, scholastic difficulties and personal problems during the period of November 11, 1957, through April 15, 1958; and

> that although said student was constantly in need of professional guidance after April 15th, 1958, said defendant suggested termination of future interviews regarding her problem; that as a result of the failure of proper guidance by said defendant as aforesaid, she suffered psychological and emotional injuries and disturbances depriving her of her own volition and resulting in death by her own hand on May 27th, 1958.

It is alleged:

That said defendant negligently and carelessly failed to perform his duties as such Director in the following:

(a) That he failed to secure or attempt to secure emergency psychiatric treatment after he was aware or should have been aware of her inability to care for the safety of herself.

(b) That he failed at all times to advise the said parents of Jeannie Bogust or contact them concerning the true mental and emotional state of their said daughter, thus preventing them from securing proper medical care for her.

(c) That he failed to provide proper student guidance.

[1] For the purposes of this decision we can assume the truth of only such allegations as are material statements of fact. Statements which are conclusions are not admitted by demurrer.

A demurrer to a complaint admits all the facts therein well pleaded, but it does not admit erroneous conclusions drawn from such facts by the pleader even though the conclusions bear the semblance of statements of fact.

[2] The first question presented on appeal is whether there is a legal duty on the part of the defendant of such nature as will sustain this action. As pointed out by the trial court, before liability can attach there must be found a duty resting upon the person against whom recovery is sought and then a breach of that duty. . . .

[3] Defendant is not a person qualified as a medical doctor or a specialist in mental disorders. It is alleged that he is an "educator by profession," a professor of education with a doctor of philosophy degree. Admitting that a teacher is not an insurer of the health, welfare and safety of his students . . . plaintiffs argue that he does have the duty to use reasonable care. . . .

b. Helplessness of other. . . . So too, a child while in school is deprived of the protection of his parents or guardian. Therefore, the actor who takes custody of . . . a child is properly required to give him the protection which the custody or the manner in which it is taken has deprived him . . .

d. Duty to anticipate danger. One who has taken custody of another may not only be required to exercise reasonable care for the other's protection when he knows or has reason to know that the other is in immediate need thereof, but also to make careful preparations to enable him to give effective protection when the need arises, and to exercise reasonable vigilance to ascertain the need of giving it . . .

The three acts of negligence with which the defendant is charged in the complaint are grounded on the theory that he had such a familiarity with and knowledge of Jeannie's problems and her "emotional disturbances, social conflicts, scholastic difficulties" that in the exercise of reasonable intelligence and judgment he should have realized her need for psychiatric treatment and acted accordingly—in securing such treatment, in advising her parents, and in providing proper guidance.

The trial court held:

To hold that a teacher who has had no training, education or experience in medical fields is required to recognize in a student a condition, the diagnosis of which is in a specialized and technical medical field, would require a duty beyond reason.

Plaintiffs allege defendant was charged with the maintenance of a counseling and testing center for various educational, vocational and personal problems which students of the college might have, but that fact does not qualify him as an expert in the field of medicine or psychiatry. Granting that he had some knowledge of Jeannie's emotional and other difficulties as the result of his meetings with her during a period of five months, as a teacher he cannot be charged with the same degree of care based on such knowledge as a person trained in medicine or psychiatry could exercise.

The first act of negligence alleged is that the defendant failed to secure psychiatric treatment for Jeannie "after he was aware or should have been aware of her inability to care for the safety of herself." This clearly implies that he should have known she had suicidal tendencies. But there is no allegation of fact that would have apprised the defendant, as a reasonably prudent man, that she had such tendencies. The statement is merely a conclusion. The same comment applies to the second act of negligence alleged, that of failing to advise the parents "thus preventing them from securing proper medical care for her." The duty of advising her parents could arise only from facts establishing knowledge on the part of defendant of a mental or emotional state which required medical care; and no such facts are alleged.

The allegation that defendant failed to provide proper student guidance apparently refers to the fact that he suggested termination of future interviews regarding her problems.

Jeannie was suffering from emotional disturbances and social conflicts before she came under defendants guidance. Plaintiffs rely on the "further harm" doctrine defined in Restatement of the Law of Torts, Vol. II, sec. 322, where it is stated, in part (Comment d, p. 872):

> The liability which this Section recognizes is not imposed as a penalty for the actor's original misconduct, but for a breach of a separate duty to aid and protect the other after his helpless condition caused by the actor's misconduct is or should be known.

There is no allegation that the interviews between the defendant and Jeannie benefited her or that there was a duty on his part to continue them or that their termination caused the injury or placed her in a worse position than she was when they were begun. . . .

One who gratuitously renders services to another, otherwise than by taking charge of him when helpless, is not subject to liability for discontinuing the services if he does not thereby leave the other in a worse position than he was in when the services were begun.

Jeannie had various problems before the interviews were undertaken, but was she "helpless" in that she was unable to look after her own safety? There is no allegation of such a fact, as pointed out above. Nor is there any allegation that she became so "helpless" during the time the interviews were carried on or that, if she did, she exhibited such manifestations as would charge the defendant with knowledge thereof.

The allegation in point is that although the deceased was in need of professional guidance after April 15, 1958, the defendant suggested termination of the interviews and that:

> as a result of the failure of proper guidance by said defendant as aforesaid, she suffered psychological and emotional injuries and disturbances depriving her of her own volition and resulting in death by her own hand on May 27, 1958.

We may assume the interviews were terminated, although the act complained of is the suggestion that they be terminated. There is no allegation that defendant's counseling caused injury. The only question is whether, at the time he suggested the interviews be terminated, he should reasonably have foreseen, acting as an ordinarily prudent and intelligent person, that as a consequence thereof Jeannie would do harm to herself, i.e. commit suicide.

In Dahlberg v. Jones, it was held that where a mental patient was under the care of a doctor in a private hospital, the degree of care owed such patient "should be in proportion to the physical and mental ailments of the patient rendering him unable to look after his own safety." In that case such a patient suffered injuries as the result of escaping from the hospital, and this court held there was no liability on the hospital where there was no evidence to support the conclusion that the doctor or the hospital staff had reasonable grounds to anticipate or to take precautions against suicide or escape. . . .

There was no evidence introduced tending to show that the deceased was possessed of suicidal mania, or mania of any kind, for that matter, at most that he was insane at intervals, but no indication whatever, prior to the fatal leap, that he intended to do himself or any one else any personal harm. In the absence of such showing there was no evidence tending to show that the defendant had any reason to anticipate that the deceased contemplated self-destruction.

Paraphrasing the above, in this case we can substitute for evidence or proof the fact that the complaint contains no allegation of a suicidal tendency or mania or any indication that Jeannie showed any disposition to injure herself.

If a hospital for the treatment of mental disorders cannot be held liable for self-injury of a patient where there is no evidence (allegation) that the patient would injure herself if not restrained, certainly the mere allegation of an awareness by a teacher of emotional disturbance and personal problems of a student is insufficient to support an action for death by suicide.

The suicide took place almost six weeks after defendant suggested terminating the interviews. The complaint alleges that Jeannie's loss of volition occurred after the interviews terminated. To hold that the termination was a negligent act, it must be alleged that defendant knew or should have known that Jeannie would commit suicide.

This is an action for wrongful death. . . . The basic theory of plaintiff's complaint and their argument on appeal is the foreseeability of Jeannie's suicide as the proximate result of defendant's acts and omissions. . . .

Where an action is brought under a wrongful death statute the general rule is that suicide constitutes an intervening force which breaks the line of causation from the wrongful act to the death and therefore the wrongful act does not render defendant civilly liable.

The only cases noted where the wrongful act is considered as within and part of the line of causation is where the wrongful act produces a rage or frenzy or uncontrollable impulse, during which state self-destruction takes place. . . . [D]ecedent had been injured by a blow on the head in a collision of his automobile with the defendant's train and the injury caused him to become insane. Two months later he took his own life. The court held:

> we are of opinion that the liability of a defendant for a death by suicide exists only when the death is the result of an uncontrollable impulse, or is accomplished in delirium or frenzy caused by the collision, and without conscious volition to produce death, having knowledge of the physical nature and consequences of the act. An act of suicide

resulting from a moderately intelligent power of choice, even though the choice is determined by a disordered mind, should be deemed a new and independent, efficient cause of the death that immediately ensues.

Plaintiffs plead that as the result of defendant's suggestion that the interviews be terminated Jeannie suffered mental injury depriving her of her own volition and resulting in her death. In the absence of any allegation of fact in that respect, the statement that her self-destruction was the result of loss of her volition is a mere conclusion. It is also significant that the complaint pleads no facts with respect to Jeannie's activities or mental condition during the period from April 15 to May 27, 1958. There are no facts alleged which, if proved, would establish a cause-effect relationship between the alleged nonfeasance of the defendant and the suicide of the deceased.

A proximate cause is one in which is involved the idea of necessity. . . . A remote cause is one which is inconclusive in reasoning, because from it no certain conclusion can be legitimately drawn. In other words, a remote cause is a cause the connection between which and the effect is uncertain, vague or indeterminate. . . . The proximate cause being given, the effect must follow. . . . The remote cause being given, the effect may or may not follow.

As a general rule a person will not be relieved of liability by an intervening force which could reasonably have been foreseen, nor by one which is a normal incident of the risk created. However, if such intervening force takes the form of suicide the practically unanimous rule is that such act is a new and independent agency which does not come within and complete a line of causation from the wrongful act to the death and therefore does not render defendant liable for the suicide.

It is pointed out in succeeding pages, in discussing cases involving the duty owned by private hospitals to their patients, that the law does not require of anyone in the exercise of reasonable care to take measures against a danger which a patient's known mental condition does not suggest as likely to happen. The test of actionable negligence in such cases is not what could have been done to prevent a particular accident but whether the hospital had notice of conduct or language evidencing a purpose to inflict self-injury.

The peculiar difficulty encountered in proving causation in a case of this kind is largely due to the nature of the subject matter. The fact that the deceased, before she came under the defendant's counsel, may already have been afflicted with a condition which would account for her suicide further complicates the issue. In discussing the reluctance of courts to extend any doctrine of recovery for mental distress alone to a situation where the defendant is charged with ordinary negligence, it is said . . . :

> The contention that because of the nature of the evidentiary problems involved, the judicial process is not well adapted to distinguishing valid from fraudulent claims in this area, has been recognized as probably the most substantial of the reasons advanced for denying recovery for mental distress or its physical consequences.
>
> A further difficulty is present in this case. Defendant is charged with three acts of negligence. Even assuming he had secured psychiatric treatment for Jeannie or that he had advised her parents of her emotional condition or that he had not suggested termination of the interviews—it would require speculation for a jury to conclude that under such circumstances she would not have taken her life.
>
> Order affirmed.

Inherent Power Theory

Esteban v. Central Missouri State College
415 Fed. 2nd. 1077
April 28, 1969.

Blackmun, Circuit Judge

Alfredo Esteban and Steve Craig Roberds, students at Central Missouri State College, a tax-supported institution at Warrensburg, Missouri, were suspended on March 31, 1967, for two semesters but with the right thereafter to apply for readmission. The two, by their next friends, instituted the present action for declaratory and injunctive relief. The named defendants are the College, its President and its Board of Regents. The plaintiffs allege primarily, First, Fifth and Fourteenth Amendment violations. Judge Hunter, with a detailed memorandum, denied them relief and dismissed their complaint.

The disciplinary action against the plaintiffs arose out of events which took place on or adjacent to the college campus on the nights of March 29 and 30, 1967. At that time Esteban was on scholastic probation and Roberds was on disciplinary probation. Esteban also had been on disciplinary probation over a knifing incident with a fellow student, but his disciplinary probation had expired a short time before.

Both sides in their appellate briefs specifically adopt findings of fact made by Judge Hunter with respect to these March, 1967 events. Accordingly, we set forth certain of those findings here:

> . . . These demonstrations took place at the intersection of the public street adjacent to the school campus and State Highway 13 and overflowed onto the sidewalks and campus. On the evening of March 29, some 350 students were present in the mass and on March 30, there were some 600 students included. As a partial result of these two mass demonstrations there was in excess of $600 damages and destruction of college property, including broken school building windows and destroyed shrubbery; eggs were thrown; the Dean of Men, Dr. Chalquist, was hanged in effigy, his "dummy" torn up and set on fire; traffic was halted and blocked, cars were rocked, and their occupants ordered out into the street. The college president directed a number of his personnel, including Dr. Meverden, to go to the scene to restore order.

ESTEBAN EVENT:

. . . The evening of March 29, 1967, around 11:30 p.m., he left his dormitory about the time the "disturbance" had subsided. Some of the students were proceeding along the street from the mass demonstration to their dormitories. Esteban proceeded down the sidewalk to within about one hundred feet of the intersection of the scene of the mass demonstration and stayed there awhile. Dr. Meverden, a faculty member, who was seeking to disperse students standing outside their dorms, approached Esteban and asked him to go inside the dormitory. Instead of complying, Esteban asked why, and on again being requested to go in, again asked why.

He told Dr. Meverden that he was not in violation of any state, county or federal law and that he had a right to be out there. Dr. Meverden asked for his student identification card, which by college regulation he was required to have in his possession at all times. Esteban said ("in rough words" according to one witness) he did not have it. Nor did he give his name. Dr. Meverden again requested him to go in the dormitory and get off the street. Esteban argued with Dr. Meverden and questioned his authority, saying there were no rules limiting the time men could stay outside the dorms. Shortly, and with the encouragement of other students present, he went into the dormitory. Dr. Meverden also went in and asked Gerald

Haddock, the resident assistant of Esteban's dormitory, who Esteban was. Esteban, as Dr. Meverden was leaving, called Haddock a prick and a bastard and told him he "would not be around very long." According to Esteban's roommate, Esteban then angrily picked up a waste can and emptied the contents on the floor at the feet of Haddock.

The college regulations in effect at the time, and to the extent pertinent, provided:

The conduct of the individual student is an important indication of character and future usefulness in life. It is therefore important that each student maintain the highest standards of integrity, honesty and morality. All students are expected to conform to ordinary and accepted social customs and to conduct themselves at all times and in all places in a manner befitting a student of Central Missouri State College.

All students that enroll at C.M.S.C. assume an obligation to abide by the rules and regulations of the college as well as all local, state and federal laws.

When a breach of regulations involves a mixed group, ALL MEMBERS ARE HELD EQUALLY RESPONSIBLE.

Conduct unbefitting a student which reflects adversely upon himself or the institution will result in disciplinary action.

Mass Gatherings—Participation in mass gatherings which might be considered as unruly or unlawful will subject a student to possible immediate dismissal from the College. Only a few students intentionally get involved in mob misconduct, but many so-called "spectators" get drawn into a fracas, and by their very presence contribute to the dimensions of the problems. It should be understood that the College considers no student to be immune from due process of law enforcement when he is in violation as an individual or as a member of a crowd.

(7) So it is here. Judge Hunter's findings have been quoted above. We have found them sufficiently supported by the record. They, too, concern an aggressive and violent demonstration and something quite apart from "peaceful, nondisruptive expression." They too, focus upon "destructive interference with the rights of others." They disclose actual or potentially disruptive conduct, aggressive action, disorder and disturbance, and acts of violence and partici-

pation therein by these plaintiffs. Their conduct, therefore, was not protected by the First and Fourteenth Amendments.

3. The regulations. These are additionally attacked for vagueness and overbreadth and hence on substantive due process grounds. Some of the loyalty oath cases are cited and it is said that the regulations' word "unlawful" is only a legal conclusion and that their references to "unruly" and "spectators" and "which might be considered" are likened to city ordinances which have been struck down when they lack sufficiency of definition. It is then argued that "young people should be told clearly what is right and what is wrong, as well as the consequences of their acts." . . . Finally, it is said that the regulations impinge and have a chilling effect upon First and Fourteenth Amendment rights.

The answers to all this, we think, are several. First, the college's regulations, per se, do not appear to us to constitute the fulcrum of the plaintiff's discomfiture. The charges against Esteban and Roberds did not even refer to the regulations. Roberds was disciplined because he had participated in the demonstrations in the face of specific warning delivered by personal interview with the dean. This was defiance of proper college authority. Esteban was disciplined because of his refusal to comply with an appropriate request by Doctor Meverden and because of his childish behavior and obscenity toward college officials. This, too, was defiance of proper college authority. There was no confusion or unawareness in either case. The exercise of common sense was all that was required. Each plaintiff knew the situation very well, knew what he was doing, and knew the consequences. Each, we might note, had had prior disciplinary experience. Their respective protestations of young and injured innocence have a hollow ring.

Secondly, we agree with Judge Hunter that it is not sound to draw an analogy between student discipline and criminal procedure, that the standard of conduct which a college seeks to impose must be one relevant to "a lawful mission, process or function of the educational institution," and that,

> . . . Certainly the regulation concerning mass demonstrations, reasonably interpreted, and as interpreted and applied by the college in the instant case to a participant in student mass demonstrations involving unlawful conduct such as the illegal blocking of a public highway and street, and the destruction of school property, is relevant to a lawful mission of the educational institution. 290 F. Supp. at 629. (footnote omitted)

(8) Thirdly, we do not find the regulation at all difficult to understand and we are positive that the college student, who is appropriately expected to possess some minimum intelligence, would not find it difficult. It asks for the adherence to standards of conduct which befit a student and it warns of the danger of mass involvement. We must assume Esteban and Roberds can read and that they possess some power of comprehension. Their difficulty was that they chose not to read or not to comprehend.

Fourthly, we see little basically or constitutionally wrong with flexibility and reasonable breadth, rather than meticulous specificity, in college regulations relating to conduct. Certainly these regulations are not to be compared with the criminal statute. They are codes of general conduct which those qualified and experienced in the field have characterized not as punishment but as part of the educational process itself and as preferably to be expressed in general rather than in specific terms. . . .

(9, 10) We agree with those courts which have held that a school has inherent authority to maintain order and to discipline students. We further agree that a school has latitude and discretion in its formulation of rules and regulations and of general standards of conduct. . . .

We regard as quite distinguishable cases such as Hammond v. South Carolina State College, 272 F. Supp. 947 (D. S. C. 1967), and Dickey v. Alabama State Bd. of Educ., supra, where the focus was on an attempted restraint of peaceful assembly or speech. Our attention has been called to the fact that Judge Doyle, in his recent opinion in Soglin v. Kauffman, 295 F. Supp. 978, 990-991 (W. D. Wis. 1968), expresses disagreement with the observations of Judge Hunter on this aspect of the case. To the extent that, in this area, Judge Doyle is in disagreement with Judge Hunter, we must respectfully disagree with Judge Doyle.

The plaintiffs are no longer children. While they may have been minors, they were beyond the age of eighteen. Their days of accomplishing ends and status by force are at an end. It was time they assumed at least the outward appearance of adulthood and of manhood. The mass denial of rights of others is irresponsible and childish. So is the defiance of proper college administrative authority ("I have the right to be here"; "I refuse to identify myself"; gutter abuse of an official; the dumping of a trash can at a resident's feet; "I plan on turning this school into a Berkeley if . . ."; and being a part of the proscribed college peace-disturbing and property-destroying demonstration). One might expect this from the spoiled child of tender years. One rightly does not expect it from the college students who has had two decades of life and who, in theory, is close to being "grown up."

(11-14) Let there be no misunderstanding as to our precise holding. We do not hold that any college regulation, however loosely framed, is necessarily valid. We do not hold that a school has the authority to require a student to discard any constitutional right when he matriculates. We do hold that a college has the inherent power to promulgate rules and regulations; that it has the inherent power properly to discipline; that it has power appropriately to protect itself and its property; that it may expect that its students adhere to generally accepted standards of conduct; that, as to these, flexibility and elbow room are to be preferred over specificity; that procedural due process must be afforded (as Judge Hunter by his first opinion here specifically required) by way of adequate notice, definite charge and a hearing with opportunity to present one's own side of the case and with all necessary protective measures; that school regulations are not to be measured by the standards which prevail for the criminal law and for criminal procedure; and that the courts should interfere only where there is a clear case of constitutional infringement.

After all, the test, we feel, is that of reasonableness. . . .

Affirmed.

CHAPTER III

The Student as a Dual Citizen:
Campus and Civic Responsibilities

R ECENT CHANGES IN THE AGE of majority as well as contemporary educational theory suggests that an increased measure of privileges and concomitant responsibilities now rest with the student-citizen.

For the first time in history, the great majority of students will assume by their attendance at a college or university, a contractual relationship. This relationship will be of particular importance in areas of contracts of enrollment and individual study, residence, service fees and charges and student activities. Educational institutions must be more careful than ever before in their catalogue description of academic, personal and vocational services offered. Administrators should not promise more that the institution is able or willing to provide. Failure to provide services to the extent of promises could result in a legal breach of contract.

The student, as well, has the added burden of complying with any agreement he may have entered into with the university. Failure to honor his assumed obligations also may result in a breach of legal contract. In both cases, however, charges should be predicated upon actual losses sustained. In many instances, charges made by the university for breached residence leases, inappropriate withdrawal from classes, and late registration are speculative in nature. Only proved loss may be recoverable and punitive fees should be avoided. For the same reason, it may be difficult for the student to successfully assert damage claims against the university for alleged failure to furnish promised services, facilities and academic enrichment.

Enrollment Contract

Whereas previously college administrators had a natural reluctance to litigate student demands for tuition refunds because the status of the claimant was that of a minor, such reluctance now seems likely to decrease given the adult status of most of the student body. Increasingly as well, students are more likely to litigate contracts of enrollment. Student claims could include improper registration, inadequate notice for changes in available courses, insufficient academic and personal counseling, and failure to make equitable assessments for course changes and withdrawals.

Residence Contracts

Residence contracts for students which previously were virtually unenforceable by the university, now take on a new dimension. Universities in many states can legally enforce legitimate claims against student residents based upon contractual agreements. Accordingly, a student will be on firm legal ground in refusing to agree to penalty clauses for the unauthorized use of residence accommodations and equipment, reservation of rights to arbitrarily inspect student rooms, unconscionable reservation and deposit fees, and nonrelated university surcharges and assessments. Universities with regulations requiring students to maintain residence must be ready to show a relationship between living on campus and the learning process. Loss of revenue, *per se,* may well be an insufficient rationale to support residence requirements for students. See *Pratz v. Louisiana Polytechnic Institute,* 28L. Ed. 541 (1971); 316 F. Supp. 872 (1970).

The resident status of those students whose parents live out of state has, of course, enormous legal implications in terms of the differential charges that a university may impose, the right of a student to vote in a municipality where he attends college, and the kinds of property insurance needs that out-of-state students may require. *Thomas Worden, et al. v. Mercer County Board of Elections,* a New Jersey Supreme Court case decided in July 14, 1972, held that all students who plan to return to their previous residences, those who plan to remain permanently in their college communities, those who plan to obtain employment away from previous residences, and those who are uncertain about their future are to be considered domiciliaries of the community in which their campus is situated, and entitled to register and vote therefrom. This holding is a dramatic departure from former precedent followed by the courts of most jurisdictions with regard to the creation of a *bona fide domicile*.

The Supreme Court of the United States in 1973 accepted for review a Connecticut controversy which involved out-of-state students who were charged higher tuition rates while attending a public institution of higher learning. The Court held that the Connecticut statute which created an irrebuttable presumption of nonresidence was violative of the Due Process Clause since no future opportunity to demonstrate bona fide residence on the part of the students was preserved. In addition to the obvious financial implications of this decision, the protection of constitutional guarantees for students may be further increased, particularly the right of an individual student to move freely from one state to another without special charges.

In terms of property rights and tort liability, insurance companies may well seize the *Worden* decision as a means to deny coverage to students completely; or to deny coverage to students who reside in a private apartment off campus. Some insurance companies, however, may continue to extend coverage to dormitory students as they have done in the past. Students, then, should be urged to confer with their respective insurance companies to ascertain whether they require additional or new coverage. This could be of significant importance to them in the event they are victimized by theft or sustain liability for personal injury to another individual.

Financial Aid

Given legal adulthood for students, financial aid officers may well have to determine the individual financial resources of students. If students are claimed for tax purposes by parents, such students could not, of course, claim independent status. Students who live at home for extended periods of time, moreover, would be precluded from declaring financial independence.

Discipline

The Fifth and Fourteenth Amendments of the United States Constitution provide for the individual against state or federal action, not against the action of private authorities. Private institutions are advised to recognize that public subsidies require state action; therefore, private institutions ultimately may feel the full impact of the Fourteenth Amendment. The fundamental concept that both public and private institutions now should understand is that the courts demand a fair hearing for those students who might be suspended. In situations where it is clear that charges asserted will not result in the suspension of a student, then requirements for procedural due process do not seem to be as necessary according to present case law. It will be to the advantage of college administrators, however, to establish campus judicial forms which include all elements of due process for all controversies, whether they involve suspension or probation.

Judicial entry into student disciplinary cases is likely to occur only where college administrators have not properly defined their rules and the way in which those rules will be implemented. The implementation of such rules must be accomplished fairly and within the objectives of institutional purpose.

A careful reading of judicial decisions in higher education indicates that both private and public institutions have the inherent authority to issue those rules necessary for the appropriate operation of their affairs. It is equally true, however, that a student cannot be precluded from various kinds of existing constitutional guarantees. Specifically, a student cannot be subject to arbitrary dismissal from an institution in which he is duly registered unless the individual's conduct was clearly disruptive of the general well-being of the university as well as violative of regulations which had been properly and clearly promulgated. *Soglin v. Kaufmann,* 295 Fed. Supp. 978 (1968), is one case where a student participated in a campus disorder and was suspended for "misconduct." University Statutes were so fundamentally ambiguous and unclear concerning "misconduct" that the court ruled that suspension was inappropriate because students could not reasonably know when they were engaging in "misconduct."

Public institutions, particularly, while having the authority to dismiss a student for good cause, nevertheless, must accord a student the rudiments of procedural due process. Due process in the case of suspension or dismissal requires that proper notice containing a statement of specific charges be provided to a student. An opportunity for a hearing also is required when a student is likely to be expelled from a university. A student, moreover, should be given the names of witnesses against him and should be given the opportunity to provide a defense against charges. Witnesses or advisors also should be available to him.

Students should be given the choice, moreover, to opt for a formal disciplinary hearing or for an informal meeting with the dean of students. A campus judicial system should permit members of the campus community to register complaints against individuals or groups with the chief student personnel officer. Complaints could come from students, faculty, deans, counsellors or any interested individuals.

If the complaint warrants adjudication, the dean of students would then meet with the accused and discuss with him disciplinary procedures and options that may be available. The accused thereby would be permitted either to accept an informal disciplinary arrangement with the dean of students or request a hearing before a campus tribunal. Procedure for further appeal should always be available. It is important, moreover, that the dean of students be able to recognize those situations which require counseling and support rather than a full-dress judicial hearing.

RELEVANT CASE MATERIALS
Enrollment Contract—Misrepresentation

The Trustees of Columbia University v. Jacobsen
148 A. 2d 63

The opinion of the court was delivered by GOLDMANN, S. J. A. D.

I

Columbia brought suit in the district court against defendant and his parents on two notes made by him and signed by them as comakers, representing the balance of tuition he owed the University. The principal due amounted to $1,049.50, but plaintiff sued for only $1,000, waiving any demand for judgment in excess of the jurisdictional limit of the court. Defendant then sought to file an answer and counterclaim demanding, among other things, money damages in the sum of $7,016. The counterclaim was in fifty counts which severally alleged that plaintiff had represented that it would teach defendant wisdom, truth, character, enlightenment, understanding, justice, liberty, honesty, courage, beauty and similar virtues and qualities; that it would develop the whole man, maturity, well-roundedness, objective thinking and the like; and that because it had failed to do so it was guilty of misrepresentation, to defendant's pecuniary damage.

II

Following a successful freshman year at Dartmouth, defendant entered Columbia University in the fall of 1951. He continued there until the end of his senior year in the spring of 1954, but was not graduated because of poor scholastic standing. Plaintiff admits the many quotations from college catalogues and brochures, inscriptions over University buildings and addressed by University officers cited in the schedules annexed to the counterclaim. The sole question is whether these statements constitute actionable misrepresentations.

[3] We are in complete agreement with the trial court that the counterclaim fails to establish the very first element, false representation, basic to any action in deceit. Plaintiff stands by every quotation relied on by defendant. Only by reading into them the imagined meanings he attributes to them can one conclude—and the conclusion would be a most tenuous, insubstantial one—that Columbia University represented it could teach wisdom, truth, justice, beauty, spirituality and all the other qualities set out in the fifty counts of the counterclaim.

A sampling from the quotations cited by defendant will suffice as illustration. Defendant quotes from a Columbia College brochure stating that:

> . . . Columbia College provides a liberal arts education . . . A liberal arts course . . . has extremely positive values of its own. Chief among these, perhaps, is something which has been a principal aim of Columbia College from the beginning: It develops the whole man. . . . [Columbia's] aim remains constant: to foster in its students a desire to learn, a habit of critical judgment, and a deep-rooted sense of personal and social responsibility. . . . [I]ts liberal arts course pursues this aim in five ways. (1) It brings you into firsthand contact with the major intellectual ideas that have helped to shape human thinking and the course of human events. (2) It gives you a broader acquaintance with the rest of

the world. (3) It guides you toward an understanding of people and their motivations. (4) It leads you to a comprehending knowledge of the scientific world. (5) It helps you acquire facility in the art of communication.

He then cites the motto of Columbia College and Columbia University: In lumine tuo videbimus lumen (In your light we shall see light), and the inscription over the college chapel: Wisdom dwelleth in the heart of him that hath understanding. He also refers to an address of the president of Columbia University at its bicentennial convocation:

> There can never have been a time in the history of the world when men had greater need of wisdom. . . . I mean an understanding of man's relationship to his fellow men and to the universe. . . . To this task of educational leadership in a troubled time and in an uncertain world, Columbia, like other great centers of learning in free societies, unhesitatingly dedicates itself.

We have thoroughly combed all the statements upon which defendant relies in his counterclaim, as well as the exhibits he handed up to the trial judge, including one of fifty-nine pages setting out his account of the circumstances leading to the present action. They add up to nothing more than a fairly complete exposition of Columbia's objectives, desires and hopes, together with factual statements as to the nature of some of the courses included in its curricula. As plaintiff correctly observes, what defendant is seeking to do is to assign to the quoted excerpts a construction and interpretation peculiarly subjective to him and completely unwarranted by the plain sense and meaning of the language used. To the defendant a college is not "Mark Hopkins at one end of a log and the student at the other," but his dream of a universal scholar cum philosopher cum humanitarian at one end of the school bench and defendant at the other.

At the heart of the defendant's counterclaim is a single complaint. He concedes that:

> I have really only one charge against Columbia: that it does not teach wisdom as it claims to do. From this charge ensues an endless number of charges, of which I have selected fifty at random. I am prepared to show that each of these fifty claims in turn is false, though the central issue is that of Columbia's pretense of teaching wisdom.

We agree with the trial judge that wisdom is not a subject which can be taught and that no rational person would accept such a claim made by any man or institution. We find nothing in the record to establish that Columbia represented, expressly or even by way of impression, that it could or would teach wisdom or the several qualities which defendant insists are "synonyms for or aspects of the same quality." The matter is perhaps best summed up in the supporting affidavit of the Dean of Columbia College, where he said:

> All that any college can do through its teachers, libraries, laboratories and other facilities is to endeavor to teach the student the known facts, acquaint him with the nature of those matters which are unknown, and thereby assist him in developing mentally, morally and physically. Wisdom is a hoped-for end product of education, experience and ability which many seek and many fail to attain.

Defendant's extended argument lacks the element of fraudulent representation indispensable to any action of deceit. We note, in passing, that he has cited no legal authority whatsoever for his position. Instead, he has submitted a dictionary definition of "wisdom" and quotations from such works as the Bhagavad-Gita, the Mundaka Upanishad, the Analects of Confucius and the Koran; excerpts from Euripides, Plato and Menander; and references to the Bible. Interesting though these may be, they do not support defendant's indictment of Columbia. If his pleadings, affidavit and exhibits demonstrate anything, it is indeed the validity of what Pope said in his Moral Essays:

> A little learning is a dangerous thing;
> Drink deep, or taste not the Pierian spring.

The papers make clear that through the years the defendant's interest has shifted from civil engineering to social work, then to physics, and finally to English and creative writing. In college he became increasingly critical of his professors and his courses; in his last year he attended classes only when he chose and rejected the regimen of examinations and term papers. When his nonattendance at classes and his poor work in the senior year were called to his attention by the Columbia Dean of Students, he replied in a lengthy letter that, "I want to learn, but I must do it my own way. I realize my behavior is nonconforming, but in these times, when there are so many forces that demand conformity, I hope I will find Columbia willing to grant some freedom to a student who wants to be a literary artist." In short, he chose to judge Columbia's educational system by the shifting standards of his own fancy, and now seeks to place his failure at Columbia's door on the theory that it had deliberately misrepresented that it taught wisdom.

III

In light of our conclusion that defendant has failed to state a cause of action in deceit based on fraudulent representation, we need not deal with plaintiff's further contentions.

Judgment affirmed.

Discipline—Fourteenth Amendment

Knight v. State Board of Education
200 Fed. Supp. 174
Dec. 16, 1961

William E. Miller, Chief Judge

In this action the plaintiffs, thirteen Negro students of Tennessee A and I State University, challenge upon constitutional grounds their suspension from the University at the end of the 1960-1961 school year. They contend that the action taken by the University, through its discipline committee, violated the plaintiffs' rights under the equal protection and due process clauses of the Fourteenth Amendment in that such action was arbitrary, discriminatory and without either notice to the plaintiffs on the charges against them or opportunity to be heard.

Pertinent and material facts in the controversy are as follows: Tennessee Agricultural and Industrial State University, located at Nashville, was organized as a college or university for Negroes, but presently is operated on an integrated basis. Its President, its operating and teaching personnel, and most of its students are members of the Negro race. It is one of the six tax-supported institutions of higher learning in the State under the general management, supervision and control of the State Board of Education. Prior to April 8, 1960, the State Board had not prescribed written or definite rules or regulations for disciplining students at the institutions under its control. Matters of discipline were largely left to each institution, although there is some evidence to indicate that there was a tacit rule or general understanding on the part of the Board that each institution would have the right to dismiss a student summarily for personal misconduct or upon being convicted of a criminal offense involving personal misconduct. Whether or not there was such an unwritten rule, it is clear from the record that it did not receive uniform interpretation by the authorities in control of the various colleges and universities under the jurisdiction of the Board, some schools acting on the assumption that the power to discipline students could be exercised without notice or any kind of hearing and other schools taking the contrary view. This was the posture on April 8, 1960, when the Tennessee Commissioner of Education, in his capacity as Chairman of the State Board of Education, addressed a letter to each of the institutions of higher learning under the Board's jurisdiction formulating a rule governing the disciplining of students for misconduct, which was later ratified and approved by the entire Board. The letter of April 8, 1960, reads as follows:

> The necessity for maintaining the integrity and honor of the student body at each of the State colleges and universities under the jurisdiction of the State Board of Education has long been recognized. The misconduct of any student enrolled in an institution of higher learning reflects dishonor and discredit upon the institution in which he is enrolled and upon higher education in general.
>
> It is for this reason, therefore, that as Chairman of the State Board of Education and acting on behalf of the Board, I am instructing you to dismiss promptly any student enrolled in the institution of which you are president who shall, in the future, be arrested and convicted on charges involving personal misconduct.
>
> This policy is to be placed into effect immediately.

The regulation so prescribed was construed by the President of Tennessee A and I as requiring prompt and mandatory suspension or dismissal of any student convicted of a criminal offense involving personal misconduct, regardless of whether such conviction may have been appealed to a higher court. This was also the construction placed upon the regulation by the authorities of other schools and by the Chairman of the State Board. The letter of April 8, 1960, was written at the time of the lunch-counter demonstrations in the City of Nashville, in which some of the plaintiffs and other Tennessee A and I students participated, protesting the prevailing practice in restaurants and at lunch counters in that city denying service to members of the Negro race. As a result of such demonstrations, many students of Tennessee A and I were arrested and convicted for alleged disorderly conduct, but the proof shows that no disciplinary action was taken by the University against any of the student participants under the regulation of April 8, 1960.

In May and June, 1961, the plaintiffs, after completion of their school work for the year, in different groups and at different times, traveled by interstate bus to Jackson, Mississippi, where they entered the waiting rooms of the Greyhound and Trailways Bus Terminals. When they refused to leave the bus terminals in response to an order from a local police officer, they were arrested, charged with disorderly conduct in violation of a Mississippi statute defining that offense, and later convicted in a Magistrate's Court. Each plaintiff received a fine of $200.00 and a sixty-day suspended jail sentence. Each plaintiff spent approximately thirty days in jail pending efforts to post an appeal bond. They were finally successful in perfecting appeals of their convictions to a higher court in Mississippi, where appeals are still pending. On June 1, 1961, a day or so after most of the convictions, but on the same day as one of the convictions and even before one of them, the discipline committee of Tennessee A and I University suspended the plaintiffs from the University after an ex parte hearing, without notice to the plaintiffs, and at a time when they were still in jail in Mississippi pending attempts to post bonds for appeals. On the same date, the committee addressed to the plaintiffs at their local residences in Nashville a letter setting forth the action of the committee as follows:

> In view of the fact that you have been arrested and convicted for violating a Mississippi law and are now in litigation to prove or disprove the validity of that arrest and conviction, and in light of the policy of the State Board of Education that provides for the dismissal of a student from a college or university under its jurisdiction when such student is arrested and convicted of charges involving misconduct, you have been placed on probation and will be denied the privilege of continuing your education at the Tennessee A and I State University. If it is later indicated that you have not violated this policy of the State Board of Education, your case may be reconsidered.

If the regulation of April 8, 1960, means that a student convicted of any criminal offense regardless of its nature and seriousness should be automatically dismissed, and if the regulation so construed should be deemed a reasonable one, then there would be merit in the defendants' argument that the discipline committee was vested with no discretion and that its sole function was to determine whether or not the plaintiffs had actually been convicted of a criminal violation. Since it is admitted that the plaintiffs were so convicted in Mississippi, notice to the plaintiffs and an opportunity to be heard before disciplinary action was taken would have served no useful purpose. But is this the correct construction of the regulations? The Court is satisfied that it is not.

In the first place, the unreasonablness of such a construction argues strongly against it. There are countless convictions for violations of the criminal law which do not necessarily reflect seriously upon the person so convicted. For example, it is inconceivable that the State Board intended in promulgating the regulation of April 8 that a minor traffic violation, such as overtime parking or running a traffic light, would subject a student to summary dismissal without any discretion whatever being vested in the schools involved. Examples of similar technical infractions could be multiplied indefinitely, and the Court cannot escape the conclusion that the State Board of Education had in mind a different meaning when the rule of April 8 was adopted. This leads to the question: What is the true meaning of the regulation?

(4) In determining this question, it would appear that the answer is supplied by the letter of April 8 when construed in its entirety. By the express language of the second paragraph, each institution under the jurisdiction of the Board was directed to dismiss promptly, not any student convicted of a criminal charge, but any student convicted on charges "involving personal misconduct." It thus appears that it is not enough for a school to determine the fact of conviction alone but it must go further and find that the charge on which the conviction is based is one which does in fact involve personal misconduct on the part of the student. It must be conceded that the term "personal misconduct" is, generally speaking, a very broad one and, if without definition for a special purpose, could embrace any type of behavior in conflict with the criminal law or even with general practice and custom. However, the term, as used in the letter of April 8, 1960, is not without definition or limitation. The term "personal misconduct" as used in the second paragraph must be interpreted in the light of the first paragraph of the same letter wherein the purpose in promulgating the regulation is stated as follows: "The misconduct of any student enrolled in an institution of higher learning reflects dishonor and discredit upon the institution in which he is enrolled and upon higher education in general." In this view the intent of the regulation was not that the schools should summarily dismiss students upon convictions of criminal offenses but only those students convicted of offenses ac-

companied by personal misconduct of a kind which reflected dishonor and discredit upon the institution. Such a construction not only meets the test of reasonableness, as it appears to the Court, but it is required by the language of the letter itself.

(5) By accepting such interpretation of the letter of April 8, the Court does not mean to imply that an institution under the jurisdiction of the State Board would necessarily be required in all cases to serve notice upon the student concerned and afford him an opportunity to be heard with respect to his actual conduct. There may be cases where the fact of conviction alone would necessarily import personal misconduct reflecting dishonor and discredit upon the institution, such as convictions for murder, rape, house-breaking and larceny, and numerous other examples which might be mentioned. But where the fact of conviction alone is not clearly indicative of personal misconduct in the sense used in the April 8 regulation, the Court is of the opinion that the due process clause of the Fourteenth Amendment, as construed by the Supreme Court, requires in the case of a state college or university notice to the student and an opportunity to be heard before the penalty of dismissal is inflicted. Otherwise, the school authorities are not in position to exercise their discretion and judgment in a fair and reasonable manner, either from the standpoint of the school or of the student. This is most certainly true as to the technical violations which the Court has already mentioned, and the Court is convinced that it is true in the present case.

(6) In this connection, it is noteworthy that the discipline committee wrote the letter of June 1, 1961, suspending the plaintiffs from school on the basis of hearsay information which they had received that the plaintiffs had been convicted in Mississippi for breach of the peace. Presumably the committee also knew that the plaintiffs had traveled to Mississippi by interstate bus in connection with the freedom rides, but when the severe penalty of suspension was imposed upon the plaintiffs, the committee did not know and had no way of knowing what the plaintiffs had actually done and what their conduct actually was in bringing about their supposed convictions upon such a general and uncertain charge as a breach of the peace. The committee did not know and had no way of knowing whether the specific conduct of each plaintiff was of such character that it reflected dishonor or discredit upon Tennessee A and I State University as required by the regulation of April 8. In brief,

the committee was not in possession of sufficient facts to enable it to exercise a fair or intelligent judgment. The necessity for a hearing in such a case is strongly emphasized by what actually occurred. As it turned out, the plaintiffs were not in fact convicted in Mississippi for a breach of the peace as the committee had supposed, but were convicted under a Mississippi Statute, Section 2087.5 of the Mississippi Code of 1942, which defines the offense of "disorderly conduct" as follows:

> Whoever with intent to provoke a breach of the peace, or under circumstances such that a breach of the peace may be occasioned thereby: (1) crowds or congregates with others in or upon . . . (naming certain public places) and who fails or refuses to disperse and move on, or disperse or move on, when ordered so to do by any law enforcement officer of any municipality, or county, in which such act or acts are committed . . . shall be guilty of disorderly conduct [emphasis added].

Under the general terms of this statute the plaintiffs were convicted on a charge that "with intent to provoke a breach of the peace" they congregated with others in or around a bus terminal in Jackson, Mississippi, and failed or refused to disperse and move on when ordered to do so by a law enforcement officer. The committee, in fact, did not even have before it the exact terms of this charge against the plaintiffs at the time they took disciplinary action. But even if the charge itself had been before the committee it would have conveyed very little information as to what the plaintiffs had actually done and at best would have left a serious doubt as to whether the plaintiffs had been guilty of such misconduct as would reflect dishonor or discredit upon the University. It is entirely conceivable under the vague and indefinite terms of the Mississippi Statute and the equally vague charge upon which the plaintiffs were convicted that they were guilty, at most, of a technical violation which the committee, if apprised of the true facts, could have decided did not call for the penalty of dismissal.

Defendants' argument that the discipline committee should not be required to go behind the convictions of a court of competent jurisdiction fails to meet the real issue. In investigating the facts attending the commission of the offense, the committee would not go behind the convictions for the purpose of determining whether they were valid or whether the students were guilty or not guilty of the offense charged, but for the purpose of determining whether the convictions, conceding their existence and validity, were for offenses actually involving the type of conduct which is aimed at by the regulation of April 8, 1960. The purpose of the investigation would be for the University to decide for itself whether there had been in fact a violation of its own disciplinary regulation.

Nothing in this opinion should be construed or taken as indicating any view on the part of the Court upon the merits of any issued to be presented to the discipline committee of the University or any view as to whether the regulation of April 8, 1960, was or was not violated by the plaintiffs or any of them.

Fourteenth Amendment—Public Institutions

Scoggin v. Lincoln University
Esteban v. Central Missouri State College

45 F. R. D. 133 (1968)
U. S. D. C., W. D. Mo., En Banc)

Memorandum on Judicial Standards of Procedure and Substance in Review of Student Discipline in Tax Supported Institutions of Higher Learning

The number of actions for review of student disciplinary action has been increasing in this and other courts. . . . (These actions) . . . reflect rapid development and much controversy concerning appropriate procedural and substantive standards of judicial review in such cases. Because of the importance in this district of clearly enunciated reliable standards, this Court scheduled hearings in the second Esteban case and in the Scoggin case for the purpose of hearing arguments and suggestions of the parties and of interested amici curiae on the standards which would be applied regardless of the judge to whom the cases are assigned by lot. This was done for the purpose of uniformity of decision in this district.

The following memorandum represents a statement of judicial standards of procedure and substance applicable, in the absence of exceptional circumstances, to actions concerning discipline of students in tax-supported educational institutions of higher learning.

. . . The modern courts are, and will continue to be, greatly indebted to higher education for their personnel, their innovations, their processes, their political support and their future in the political and social order. Higher education is the primary source of study and support of improvement in the courts. For this reason, among others, the courts should exercise caution when importuned to intervene in the important processes and functions of education. A court should never intervene in the processes of education without understanding the nature of education.

Before undertaking to intervene in the educational processes, and to impose judicial restraints and mandates on the educational community, the courts should acquire a general knowledge of the lawful missions and the continually changing processes, functions and problems of education. Judicial action without such knowledge would endanger the public interest and be likely to lead to gross injustice.

Education is the living and growing source of our progressive civilization, of our open repository of increasing knowledge, culture and our salutary democratic traditions. As such, education deserves the highest respect and the fullest protection of the courts in the performance of its lawful missions.

There have been, and no doubt in the future there will be, instances of erroneous and unwise misuse of power by those invested with powers of management and teaching in the academic community, as in the case of all human fallible institutions. When such misuse of power is threatened or occurs, our political and social order has made available a wide variety of lawful, nonviolent, political, economic and social means to prevent or end the misuse of power. These same lawful, nonviolent, political, economic and social means are available to correct an unwise, but lawful choice of educational policy or action by those charged with the powers of management and teaching in the academic community. Only where the erroneous and unwise actions in the field of education deprive students of federally-protected rights or privileges does a federal court have power to intervene in the educational process.

The tax-supported educational institution is an agency of the national and state governments. Its missions include, by teaching, research and action, assisting in the declared purposes of government in this nation.

The nihilist and the anarchist, determined to destroy the existing political and social order, who directs his primary attack on the educational institutions, understands fully the mission of education in the United States.

Federal law recognizes the powers of the tax-supported institutions to accomplish these missions and has frequently furnished economic assistance for these purposes.

If it is true, as it well may be, that man is in a race between education and catastrophe, it is imperative that educational institutions not be limited in the performance of their lawful missions by unwarranted judicial interference.

Attendance at a tax-supported educational institution of higher learning is not compulsory. The federal constitution protects the equality of opportunity of all qualified persons to attend. Whether this protected opportunity be called a qualified "right" or "privilege" is unimportant. It is optional and voluntary.

The voluntary attendance of a student in such institutions is a voluntary entrance into the academic community. By such voluntary entrance, the student voluntarily assumes obligations of performance and behavior reasonably imposed by the institution of choice relevant to its lawful missions, processes and functions. These obligations are generally much higher than those imposed on all citizens by the civil and criminal law. So long as there is no deprival of due process, no abridgement of a right protected in the circumstances, and no capricious, clearly unreasonable or unlawful action employed, the institution may discipline students to secure compliance with these higher obligations as a teaching method or to sever the student from the academic community.

No student may, without liability to lawful discipline, intentionally act to impair or prevent the accomplishment of any lawful mission, process or function of an educational institution.

The discipline of students in the educational community is, in all but the case of irrevocable expulsion, a part of the teaching process. In the case of irrevocable expulsion for misconduct, the process is not punitive or deterrent in the criminal law sense, but the process is rather the determination that the student is unqualified to continue as a member of the educational community. Even then, the disciplinary process is not equivalent to the criminal law processes of federal and state criminal law. For, while the expelled student may suffer damaging effects, sometimes irreparable, to his educational, social and economic future, he or she may not be imprisoned, fined, disenfranchised or subjected to probationary supervision. The attempted analogy of student discipline to criminal proceedings against adults and juveniles is not sound.

In the lesser disciplinary procedures, including, but not limited to, guidance counseling, reprimand, suspension of social or academic privileges, probation, restriction to campus and dismissal with leave to apply for readmission, the lawful aim of discipline may be teaching in performance of a lawful mission of the institution. The nature and procedures of the disciplinary process in such cases should not be required to conform to federal processes of criminal law, which are far from perfect, and designed for circumstances and ends unrelated to the academic community in student discipline; the intricate, time-consuming, sophisticated procedures, rules and safeguards of criminal law would frustrate the teaching process and render the institutional control impotent.

A federal court should not intervene to reverse or enjoin disciplinary actions relevant to a lawful mission of an educational institution unless there appears one of the following:

(1) a deprival of due process, that is, fundamental concepts of fair play;

(2) invidious discrimination, for example, on account of race or religion;

(3) denial of federal rights, constitutional or statutory, protected in the academic community; or

(4) clearly unreasonable, arbitrary or capricious action.

Equal opportunity for admission and attendance by qualified persons at tax-supported state educational institutions of higher learning is protected by the equal privileges and immunities, equal protection of laws, and due process clauses of the Fourteenth Amendment to the United States Constitution. . . . It is unimportant whether this protected opportunity is defined as a right or a privilege. The protection of the opportunity is the important thing.

In the field of discipline, scholastic and behavioral, an institution may establish any standards reasonably relevant to the lawful missions, processes and functions of the institution. It is not a lawful mission, process or function of an institution to prohibit the exercise of a right guaranteed by the Constitution or a law of the United States to a member of the academic community under the circumstances. Therefore, such prohibitions are not reasonably relevant to any lawful mission, process or function of an institution.

Standards so established may apply to student behavior on and off campus when relevant to any lawful mission, process or function of the institution. By such standards of student conduct the institution may prohibit any action or omission which impairs, interferes with, or obstructs the missions, processes and functions of the institution.

Standards so established may require scholastic attainments higher than the average of the population and may require superior ethical and moral behavior. In establishing standards of behavior, the institution is not limited to the standards or the forms of criminal law.

An institution may establish appropriate standards of conduct (scholastic and behavioral) in any form and manner reasonably calculated to give adequate notice of the scholastic attainments and behavior expected of the student.

The notice of the scholastic and behavioral standards to the students may be written or oral, or partly written and partly oral, but preferably written. The standards may be positive or negative in form.

Outstanding educational authorities in the field of higher education believe, on the basis of experience, that detailed codes of prohibited student conduct are provocative and should not be employed in higher education.

For this reason, general affirmative statements of what is expected of a student may in some areas be preferable in higher education. Such affirmative standards may be employed, and discipline of students based thereon.

The legal doctrine that a prohibitory statute is void if it is overly broad or unconstitutionally broad does not, in the absence of exceptional circumstances, apply to standards of student conduct. The validity of the form of standards of student conduct, relevant to the lawful missions of higher education, ordinarily should be determined by recognized educational standards.

In severe cases of student discipline for alleged misconduct, such as final expulsion, indefinite or long-term suspension, dismissal with deferred leave to reapply, the institution is obligated to give to the student minimal procedural requirements of due process of law. The requirements of due process do not demand an inflexible procedure for all such cases. . . . Three minimal requirements apply in cases of severe discipline, growing out of fundamental conceptions of fairness implicit in procedural due process. First, the student should be given adequate notice in writing of the specific ground or grounds and the nature of the evidence on which the disciplinary proceedings are based. Second, the student should be given an opportunity for a hearing in which the disciplinary authority provides a fair opportunity for hearing of the student's position, explanations and evidence. The third requirement is that no disciplinary action be taken on grounds which are not supported by any substantial evidence. Within limits of due process, institutions must be free to devise various types of disciplinary procedures relevant to their lawful missions, consistent with their varying processes and functions, and not an unreasonable strain on their resources and personnel.

There is no general requirement that procedural due process in student disciplinary cases provide for legal representation, a public hearing, confrontation and cross-examination of witnesses, warnings about privileges, self-incrimination, application of principles of former or double jeopardy, compulsory production of witnesses or any of the remaining features of federal criminal jurisprudence. Rare and exceptional circumstances, however, may require provision of one or more of these features in a particular case to guarantee the fundamental concepts of fair play.

It is encouraging to note the current unusual efforts of the institutions and the interested organizations which are devising and recommending procedures and policies in student discipline which are based on standards, in many features, far higher than the requirements of due process.

Fourteenth Amendment—Private Institutions

Richard Zerbo v. Drew University

United States District Court
District of New Jersey
August 10, 1973
Coolahan, District Judge

This is a civil rights action brought by a Drew University student who has been indefinitely suspended for having violated certain university regulations. The plaintiff, Richard J. Zerbo, brings this action pursuant to 42 U.S.C. §1983. He seeks a preliminary mandatory injunction ordering the defendants, President Robert Oxnam

---

2. (A delineation of due process requirements may be found in Title 42, U.S.C.A., Section 1983.)

and the Trustees of Drew University, to immediately reinstate him as a full-time student. The defendants move to dismiss the action on the grounds that this court lacks jurisdiction.

The Court will deny the plaintiff's motion for a preliminary injunction, and will grant the defendants' motion to dismiss the action for lack of jurisdiction.

On January 31, 1973, Richard J. Zerbo, the plaintiff in this matter, was arrested in the Borough of Chatham, New Jersey, by police officers of that municipality and charged with possession with intent to distribute controlled dangerous substances, to wit, marijuana and hashish, in violation of N.J.S.A. 24:19-21. On March 13, 1973, a criminal indictment was returned against Mr. Zerbo by the Morris County Grand Jury, upon which indictment he is presently awaiting trial.

At the time of his arrest Mr. Zerbo was enrolled as a full-time student in Drew University, an institution of higher learning located in Madison, New Jersey. After Drew University officials were informed that criminal charges had been filed against Mr. Zerbo in the Borough of Chatham, Dean Inez G. Nelback advised him that the criminal charges lodged against him constituted a violation of university regulations. Dean Nelback also informed Mr. Zerbo that he could voluntarily withdraw from the university pending the outcome of his trial, as an alternative to his being indefinitely suspended. Mr. Zerbo apparently did not exercise his right to withdraw voluntarily, and on February 12, 1973, he was indefinitely suspended by order of Dr. Robert Oxnam, President of Drew University.

On March 21, 1973, the plaintiff brought this action seeking a preliminary injunction ordering his reinstatement as a full-time student at Drew University.

The plaintiff asserts that his suspension from Drew University violated his constitutional rights to a fair and impartial hearing, a presumption of innocence, confrontation of witnesses, representation by counsel, equal protection of the laws, and substantive and procedural due process. The plaintiff further alleges that the disciplinary rules and regulations governing suspensions and/or expulsions of students from Drew University are so vague and indefinite as to be void and of no force and effect. The plaintiff also claims that his suspension was a direct and proximate result of his "anti-administration" activities as co-editor of a student newspaper.

There is no need to consider any of the plaintiff's constitutional claims on the merits since I find that the actions of the defendants in suspending and refusing to reinstate the plaintiff were not done "under color of any State law, statute, ordinance, regulation, custom or usage," as required by Title 42, Section 1983 of the United States Code, and this Court therefore has no jurisdiction to decide this dispute.

Under the provisions of the Civil Rights Act of 1871, 42 U. S. C. §1983, the jurisdiction of federal courts to hear complaints of the type here presented is limited to deprivations of constitutional rights made under color of any state law, statute, ordinance, regulation, custom or usage. Therefore, no jurisdiction exists over the acts of "private" individuals and institutions absent a showing of a significant state involvement or "state action" in the challenged activities.

On the one hand, it is clear that the federal district courts do have jurisdiction to entertain and determine civil rights actions brought by students who claim their constitutional rights have been violated during the course of admission, suspension or expulsion proceedings involving tax-supported "public" institutions of higher learning.

On the other hand, it is also clear that the federal district courts have no jurisdiction to hear and determine disputes involving the power of nontax-supported "private" institutions of higher learning to suspend or expel students for disciplinary infractions or for academic deficiencies.

There is, however, no precise judicial formula for determining whether "state involvement" may exist in the affairs of a purportedly "private" university, nor for determining how extensive such "state involvement" must be in order for an action to meet the jurisdictional requirements of 42 U. S. C. §1983. Such determinations depend upon the flexible judicial process of "sifting facts and weighing circumstances," in an effort to discover whether the State has "insinuated itself into the affairs of the University in such a way that the University's conduct cannot be considered to be so purely private as to fall without the scope of the Fourteenth Amendment."

The plaintiff in this suit claims that "state action" was involved in his suspension from Drew University, alleging in his Complaint that Drew University is an "arm and instrumentality of the State of New Jersey engaged in state action." Neither the facts nor the law would appear to support this allegation.

Drew University is an institution of higher learning with its principal campus located at Madison, New Jersey. Although Drew University does operate by virtue of a charter of incorporation granted by the State of New Jersey, it nonetheless purports to be a private nonprofit institution which functions free of any significant interdependence with the State of New Jersey. There is in fact no statute in New Jersey designating Drew University as an instrumentality of the State, nor is there any statute designating Drew University as a State-related institution of higher learning. Neither is the conferring and bestowing of degrees by Drew University subject to review by the State of New Jersey, nor are any of the officials or trustees of Drew University designated or appointed by the State of New Jersey.

The plaintiff argues that because Drew University furnishes educational, cultural and intellectual opportunities to students and to the surrounding community it engages in "state action," in that such activities serve a "public purpose and function." To support his position the plaintiff cites as authority Belk v. Chancellor of Washington University, 336 F. Supp. 45 (E. D. Mo. 1970). In that particular case certain students of a private university sought an injunction ordering the university Chancellor to exercise his power to prevent repeated disruptions in classes and educational activities by student protests and demonstrations. The plaintiffs claimed that they had been denied their right to participate in the educational institution to which they were entitled to attend under conditions conducive to education, and that refusal of the Chancellor to act constituted "state action" in violation of the due process clause of the Fourteenth Amendment. In denying the defendant's motion to dismiss the action for lack of jurisdiction the district court stated "that the conduct of the chief executive of a private university, in light of the public function of a private university in education, could amount to sufficient 'state action' in order to grant jurisdiction to this court. It now remains for the plaintiffs at the trial to prove such allegations as would confer the necessary jurisdiction."

The Belk case is clearly distinguishable from the type of action now before this Court. Belk dealt with the issue of whether the alleged failure or refusal of a private university official to exercise his "state-granted" (Charter) authority to preserve and protect the orderliness of the educational process amounted to "state action." Here, this Court must decide whether the disciplinary power exercised by a private university official in suspending a student amounts to "state action." Furthermore, although the court in Belk emphasized "that the private ownership or operation of a facility with a public interest does not automatically insulate it from the commands of the Fourteenth Amendment," most courts have unqualifiedly rejected the argument that the furnishing of higher education by a private institution necessarily constitutes state action because it is a "public function."

The plaintiff next contends that state involvement exists in the affairs of Drew University by the fact that Drew enjoys tax-exempt status. However, there is no evidence in the record to indicate that this alleged financial "benefit" of tax-exempt status is or can be utilized by the State of New Jersey to dictate or influence the general affairs of Drew University or, most importantly, the specific disciplinary activities which the plaintiff is challenging in this suit. Consequently, this court agrees with the Tenth Circuit's holding in Browns v. Mitchell that tax-exemptions which have no bearing on the challenged actions beyond the perpetuation of the educational institution itself fall far short of the requisite State involvement to sustain jurisdiction under 42 U. S. C. §1983.

The plaintiff also alleges that Drew University is in "substantial part tax-supported," in that it receives, is allotted and is the beneficiary of financial aid from the State of New Jersey, and that Drew educates certain students who are recipients of New Jersey state scholarships and other financial aid directly derived from the State of New Jersey.

The facts on the record do not support the plaintiff's claim that Drew University is in substantial part tax-supported. The total amount of financial aid which both Drew University and Drew University students received from the State of New Jersey during the last fiscal year (July 1, '72-'73) was approximately $302,167.00, which amount represents less than 4 percent of Drew's total budget of $7,857,314.00. These minimal outright grant-in-aid monies from the State of New Jersey are not sufficient to transform Drew University into a "substantially" tax-supported institution. Brownley v. Gettysburg College, 338 F. Supp. 725 (M. D. Pa. 1972).

The Court is cognizant of the fact that in some instances grants-in-aid by a state to a private educational institution, regardless of the amount of such aid, may afford a jurisdictional ground for a federal district court to hear a constitutional complaint charging racial or religious discrimination. Cooper v. Aaron, 358 U. S. 1, 19 (1958); Louisiana Education Comm'n v. Poindexter, 393 U. S. 17, aff'g 296 F. Supp. 686 (E. D. La. 1968). However, such is not the case now before this Court. This plaintiff is not challenging Drew University on racial or religious discrimination grounds. The plaintiff is only challenging the internal disciplinary activities of Drew and the alleged lack of due process involved in his indefinite suspension. Under these circumstances the Court agrees with Judge Friendly's statement, writing for the Second Circuit in Grafton v. Brooklyn Law School, that "while a grant or other index of state involvement may be impermissible when it 'fosters or encourages' discrimination on the basis of race, the same limited involvement may not rise to the level of 'state action' when the action in question is alleged to affront other constitutional rights."

The fact that the State of New Jersey is involved to a de minimus degree in the financial affairs of Drew University is not sufficient to justify a finding that "state action" exists in this particular suit. In any event, the plaintiff has failed to show that the grant-in-aid-monies which Drew University receives from the State of New Jersey are in any way, shape or form applied towards financing the internal disciplinary activities which he is now challenging. The critical test in determining if "state action" is present is not whether the State of New Jersey is involved simply with some activity of Drew University, unrelated to the plaintiff's injury, but whether the State of New Jersey is directly and substantially involved with the specific activity that caused the plaintiff's injury.

Lastly, the plaintiff alleges that because the police force of the Borough of Madison, an arm and instrumentality of the State of New Jersey, was and is "substantially involved" in the internal disciplinary affairs of Drew University, his suspension involved "state action."

While the plaintiff's argument might conceivably have some merit under a different set of circumstances, it is clearly not responsive to the particular facts presented in this suit.

First, the plaintiff's suspension from Drew University did not arise from any local Madison police activity occurring on the Drew University campus. He was in fact arrested off-campus in the Borough of Chatham by police officers of that municipality. The plaintiff has not presented any evidence tending to show that Drew University officials in any way collaborated with the Chatham police in causing this arrest.

Second, it is clear that a student arrested and charged with a narcotics offense violates the established rules and regulations of Drew University. The plaintiff has not presented any evidence tending to show that the State of New Jersey, through local police forces, controls or dictates the rules, regulations or disciplinary policies of Drew University. See Blackburn v. Fisk University.

Third, the President of Drew University, exercising the discretionary power delegated him by the Charter and Trustees, and acting upon the recommendation of the Dean of the College of Liberal Arts, decided to indefinitely suspend the plaintiff. The plaintiff has not presented any evidence tending to show that the State of New Jersey, through local police forces, coerced or controlled the President's decision. Neither is there any evidence tending to show that in suspending the plaintiff the President and Trustees of Drew University were performing any duty imposed upon them by state law, or made any pretense that they were acting under state law. See Robinson v. Davis, 447 F. 2d 753 (4 Cir. 1971).

After hearing oral argument and reviewing and weighing all of the facts and circumstances presented on the record and in the briefs, and after having examined the relevant case law authorities, I find that the plaintiff has failed to show that the State of New Jersey "has so far insinuated itself into a position of interdependence" with Drew University that it must be recognized as a "joint participant in the challenged activity." Burton v. Wilmington Parking Authority; Braden v. University of Pittsburgh. There being no "state action" involved in the plaintiff's suspension from Drew University, there is no federal jurisdiction over this matter.

The defendant's motion to dismiss the complaint will be granted. Let an appropriate order be submitted.

CHAPTER IV

Students, Drugs and the Law — Case Study and Materials

THE INCREASING USE of mood-altering drugs and controlled dangerous substances by Americans in general, and students in particular, continues to cause substantial concern to college administrators. This concern obviously has both educational and legal implications.

Student drug users are not all long-haired and sandal-footed. They are as varied as the backgrounds from which they come. No one method of analysis enables the educator to understand and effectively deal with students and their involvement with drugs. Much has been written about college drug users, i.e. why drugs are taken, who takes them, and what can be done in terms of preventing continued use. Important as it is for the educator to be sensitive to such questions, a virtually unexplored sector of his responsibility deals with the effects of student illegal drug use upon the following relationships:

1. The civil liability of the college to students
2. The civil liability of student to fellow student

The use of drugs by college students is a comparatively recent phenomenon and, therefore, there has been a paucity of cases delineating the parameters of university liability for self-inflicted injuries suffered by student drug users.

The cases which research does disclose have been predicated upon the narrow and constricted classical theory of university function, i.e. the university is an institution solely for the advancement of knowledge and learning. In those cases where students have contributed to their own injury, the courts have not held the university liable and have presumed that students are sufficiently mature to conduct their own personal affairs. Lowering the age of majority in many states has reinforced this presumption. No cases apparently require the university or its employees to assume any duty of regulating the private lives of students or directing the operation of student clubs and associations.

In a number of cases, parents of students have complained that universities in which their children are enrolled have permitted their sons and daughters to become, among other things, drug users. Invariably, the courts have dismissed such claims, asserting that it is not the university's obligation to supervise a student's private life in keeping with the accelerating demise of *in loco parentis*. However, it should be noted that future case law may depart from previous judicial interpretations of university liability. Indeed, the pressures of public policy may require a university and its employees to take appropriate action when there is knowledge of regular drug use by a student.

A second category of liability would be where a student asserts a claim against the university because of injuries inflicted by a fellow student while under the influence of drugs. Here, the basic tenets of tort-negligence law are applicable. If the university has acted in an unreasonable manner or failed to act, negligence can be asserted. In these instances, it must be first shown that the university had actual or constructive notice of illegal drug use by the offending student. It must be further shown that the college could have reasonably foreseen that an injury was likely to have been inflicted by the offending student. This vicious propensity doctrine is a general rule of tort law utilized in other circumstances. College administrators, upon becoming aware of violent conduct on the part of particular student drug users, should immediately take steps to isolate such conduct.

In a recent New Jersey case, *State in the Interest of G. C.,* 121 New Jersey Superior 108 (1972), the court held that where there was reason to believe that a public school student was in illegal possession of and selling dangerous drugs, a "fair" search could be undertaken. At issue in this case was a fundamental but recurring conflict, a student's right to privacy, versus the affirmative obligation of school authorities to investigate the charge that a particular student is using or possesses narcotics.

It is, of course, well established that the Fourth Amendment protects individuals against unreasonable search and seizure. In *Re Gault,* 387 U. S. 187 S. Ct. 1428, (1967), held that neither the

Fourteenth Amendment nor the Bill of Rights is for adults alone. Children also are entitled to the constitutional safeguards of due process of law. Building upon the *Gault* foundation, the U. S. Supreme Court emphasized in *Tinker V. Des Moines Independent School District,* 393 U. S. 503, 89 S. Ct. 733 (1969), that a student does not leave his constitutional protection at the school house door. Whether a school administration is acting "insolently" in investigating allegations that a student is in possession of and selling dangerous drugs is a fact question that goes with the reasonableness of the search. It is well to remember, however, that when a reasonable search is not performed, the pain of such omission may be felt not by the administrator but by the offender's next victim.

The Fourth Amendment, however, only restrains the actions of a so-called governmental official. Such officials, in performing their assigned duties, are not only subject to the restraints of the Bill of Rights and the inhibitions of the Fourth Amendment, but also to the right of privacy as articulated in *Mapp v. Ohio,* 367 U. S. 643, 81 Sup. Ct. 1684 (1961) i.e. any evidence illegally seized in the exercise of a public official's duties would be inadmissable in an ensuing criminal state or federal prosecution. Many jurisdictions have accepted the proposition that a public school administrator is a governmental official to which constitutional limitations mentioned above might apply.

Administrators of public colleges and universities are generally subject to the same limitations described in *State in the Interest of G. C.* These limitations are not apparent for administrators of private institutions who under most circumstances would not be considered governmental officials. The question that remains may be stated in this fashion, i.e. given reasonable suspicion, is the charge of illegal drug possession and sale by a private university student sufficient to justify an administrative search in order to safeguard student health and maintain an orderly academic environment? If a student, of course, knowingly and freely consents to such a search, he cannot later successfully challenge the fruits of that search as having been obtained illegally.

The private college administrator has considerably more latitude in deciding what is good and reasonable cause for the search of student premises. He may, in certain situations, especially where dangerous and addictive drugs are involved, have the affirmative obligation to investigate and search. Private college administrators, moreover, are cautioned against overzealousness on the one hand, and insouciance on the other.

Confidentiality of communication between student and administrator is not generally privileged by law. However, in most states the law recognizes the confidentiality of communications between the following: priest and penitent; newspaperman and source; attorney and client; physician and patient; and more recently in some states, certified psychologist and client. If a college administrator acts in the capacity of legal counsel, psychologist, physician or clergyman, communications with a student on drugs or related matters are privileged. It is important to realize, however, that such privileges may not be absolute, particularly in cases concerning addictive substances. The N. Y. State Uniform Narcotics Drug Act, for example, specifically provides that "no communications made to a physician shall be deemed confidential within the meaning of the provision of the Civil Practice Act relating to confidential communications between physicians and patients." The same law also stipulates: "Information communicated to a physician or dentist in an effort unlawfully to procure a narcotic drug, or unlawfully to procure the administration of such drug, shall not be deemed a privileged communication."

It is well to note that few administrators, when advising students, act in the capacity of priest or legal counsel, even if in fact they have such credentials. Students should be warned when consulting with such administrators that their communications may not be privileged.

RELEVANT CASE MATERIAL
Fourth Amendment—Search and Seizure
Moore v. Student Affairs Committee of Troy State University
284 F. Supp. 725
May 14, 1968

Johnson, Chief Judge

On February 28, 1968, plaintiff, Gregory Gordon Moore, was a student in good standing at Troy State University and resided in a dormitory on the campus which he rented from the school. A search of his room on that day, conducted by the Dean of Men and two agents of the State of Alabama Health Department, Bureau of Primary Prevention, in plaintiff's presence, revealed a substance which, upon analysis, proved to be marijuana. Following a hearing on March 27, 1968, by the Student Affairs Committee of Troy State University, plaintiff was "indefinitely suspended" from that institution on March 28.

This action was commenced on March 30, 1968, seeking reinstatement of plaintiff as a student in good standing. At a hearing in this court conducted on April 26, 1968, it was determined that plaintiff had exhausted his administrative remedies at Troy State University and that he "was denied his right to procedural due process of law in the hearing conducted at Troy State University on March 27, 1968, as a result of which he was indefinitely suspended." On motion of the defendants, jurisdiction of this cause was retained pending remand to the Student Affairs Committee of Troy State University for the purpose of conducting a hearing comporting with procedural due process of law. Pending those proceedings, plaintiff was ordered reinstated.

(1) On May 1, 1968, a second hearing was held before the Student Affairs Committee and plaintiff was again indefinitely suspended. He again challenges, from a procedural point of view, the action taken in suspending him. He does not challenge the underlying substantive basis for the action of the Student Affairs Committee. If the plaintiff, while a student, possessed marijuana in a dormitory on campus in violation of state law, then indefinite suspension from his status as a student is clearly justified.

(2) Plaintiff now seeks relief in this court. First, he seeks readmission as a student at Troy State University on the ground of denial of procedural due process in the proceedings which resulted in his suspension; second, he seeks a declaratory judgment that none of the evidence seized in the search of his room "may be admitted in any criminal proceedings . . . ;" and third, he alleges the admission in the University's hearing of the evidence obtained through a search of his dormitory room violates his Fourth Amendment rights prohibiting illegal search and seizure. The second part of the relief sought is clearly unavailable.

On the morning of February 28, 1968, the Dean of Men of Troy State University was called to the office of the Chief of Police of Troy, Alabama, where a conference was held regarding "the possibility of there being marijuana on the campus." Two narcotics agents, the chief of police and two students were present. A second meeting was held later that morning at which a list was procured of the names of students whose rooms the officers desired permission to search. This information came from unnamed but reliable informers. About 1:00 p.m., the officers received additional information that some of the subjects they were interested in were packing to leave the campus for a break following the end of the examination period. Upon receipt of this information, and fearing a "leak," two narcotics agents, accompanied by the Dean of Men, searched six dormitory rooms in two separate residence halls. The search of the room which plaintiff occupied alone occurred between approximately 2:30 and 2:45 p.m., in his presence, but without his permission.

At the second hearing before the Student Affairs Committee, the following stipulation was entered concerning the search:

That no search warrant was obtained in this case, that no consent to search was given by the defendant, that the search was not incidental to a legal arrest, that no other offense was committed by the defendant in the arresting officers' presence, that Troy State University had in force and effect at the time of the search and subsequent arrest of the defendant the following regulation,

"The college reserves the right to enter rooms for inspection purposes. If the administration deems it necessary the room may be searched and the occupant required to open his personal baggage and other personal material which is sealed."

This language appears in the Troy State current bulletin of the year 1967-68. The quoted language also appears . . . in the Troy State Bulletin for the year 1967-68. . . . This language also appears in the current publication of the Oracle, which is a student handbook. . . . This language further appears on the reverse side of a leaflet entitled "Residence Hall Policies" which is also made available to all students of Troy State University.

It is further stipulated that the defendant's room was searched at the invitation or consent of Troy State University by the law enforcement officials acting under the above-quoted regulations.

The search revealed a matchbox containing a small amount of vegetable matter, which a state toxicologist who examined it testified was marijuana. All this testimony was received over plaintiff's objection that the evidence was seized as a result of a search in violation of the Fourth Amendment. He also challenges the constitutionality, facially and as applied, of the regulation under which the search was conducted.

This Court has previously expressed itself on the question of campus regulations, and the duty of school administrations to maintain order and discipline on their campuses in an environment suited to education, in Dickey v. Alabama State Board of Education, 273 F. Supp. 613, 617-618.

This Court recognizes that the establishment of an educational program requires certain rules and regulations necessary for maintaining an orderly program and operating the institution in a manner conductive to learning. However, the school and school officials have always been bound by the requirement that the rules and regulations must be reasonable. Courts may only consider whether rules and regulations that are imposed by school authorities are a reasonable exercise of the power and discretion vested in those authorities. Regulations and rules which are necessary in maintaining order and discipline are always considered reasonable. . . . State school officials cannot infringe on their students' right of free and unrestricted expression as guaranteed by the Constitution of the United States where the exercise of such right does not "materially and substantially interfere with requirements of appropriate discipline in the operation of the school."

(5-9) College students who reside in dormitories have a special relationship with the college involved. Insofar as the Fourth Amendment affects that relationship, it does not depend on either a general theory of the right of privacy or on traditional property concepts. The college does not stand, strictly speaking, in loco parentis to its students, nor is their relationship purely contractual in the traditional sense. The relationship grows out of the peculiar and sometimes the seemingly competing interests of college and student. A student naturally has the right to be free of unreasonable search and seizures, and a tax-supported public college may not compel a "waiver" of that right as a condition precedent to admission. The college, on the other hand, has an "affirmative obligation" to promulgate and to enforce reasonable regulations designed to protect campus order and discipline and to promote an environment consistent with the educational process. The validity of the regulation authorizing search of dormitories thus does not depend on whether a student "waives" his right to Fourth Amendment protection or on whether he has "contracted" it away; rather, its validity is determined by whether the regulation is a reasonable exercise of the college's supervisory duty. In other words, if the regulation, or, in the absence of a regulation, the action of the college authorities, is necessary in aid of the basic responsibility of the institution regarding discipline and the maintenance of an "educational atmosphere," then it will be presumed facially reasonable despite the fact that it may infringe to some extent on the outer bounds of the Fourth Amendment rights of students.

(10-12) In Englehart v. Serena, a civil action for alleged wrongful expulsion, the Supreme Court of Missouri defined the dormitory student-college relationship in real property terms as follows:

> One of the grounds on which appellant seeks a recovery of damages is that he was deprived of the "possession" of the room he was occupying in the dormitory before the expiration of the period for which he had paid "rent." He was not, however, a tenant in any sense of the word. He did not have even the full and unrestricted rights of a lodger, because Albert Hall was not an ordinary lodging house. It was an auxiliary of the college, and was maintained and conducted in furtherance of that institution's general purposes. When appellant took up residence there, he impliedly agreed to conform to all reasonable rules and regulations for its government which were then in force or which might thereafter be adopted by the proper authorities.

That definition is equally apt when measuring the relationship of this plaintiff and Troy State University by the Fourth Amendment. The student is subject only to reasonable rules and regulations, but his rights must yield to the extent that they would interfere with the institution's fundamental duty to operate the school as an educational institution. A reasonable right of inspection is necessary to the institution's performance of that duty even though it may infringe on the outer boundaries of a dormitory student's Fourth Amendment rights. . . . The regulation of Troy State University in issue here is thus facially reasonable.

(13, 14) The regulation was reasonably applied in this case. The constitutional boundary line between the right of the school authorities to search and the right of a dormitory student to privacy must be based on a reasonable belief on the part of the college authorities that a student is using a dormitory room for a purpose which is illegal or which would otherwise seriously interfere with campus discipline. Upon this submission, it is clear that such a belief existed in this case.[3]

(15-16) This standard of "reasonable cause to believe" to justify a search by college administrators—even where the sole purpose is to seek evidence of suspected violations of law—is lower than the constitutionally protected criminal law standard of "probably cause." This is true because of the special necessities of the student-college relationship and because college disciplinary proceedings are not criminal proceedings in the constitutional sense. It is clearly settled that due process in college disciplinary proceedings does not require full-blown adversary hearings subject to rules of evidence and all constitutional criminal guaranties. "Such a hearing, with the attending publicity and disturbance of college activities, might be detrimental to the college's educational atmosphere and impractical to carry out." ...

(17, 18) Assuming that the Fourth Amendment applied to college disciplinary proceedings, the search in this case would not be in violation of it. It is settled law that the Fourth Amendment does not prohibit reasonable searches when the search is conducted by a superior charged with a responsibility of maintaining discipline and order or of maintaining security. A student who lives in a dormitory on campus which he "rents" from the school waives objection to any reasonable searches conducted pursuant to reasonable and necessary regulations such as this one.

(19) Plaintiff also alleges that he was denied procedural due process of law in the hearing in that the hearing was not open to the press, other students and the public generally. Pursuant to a long-standing policy of the school, the hearing was attended only by the Student Affairs Committee—whose membership contains two students—the witnesses, plaintiff and his counsel, and plaintiff's parents. Over the plaintiff's objection, a newspaper reporter was forbidden to attend, but a full record of the proceedings was made by a court reporter.

(20, 21) This Court has recently expressed its opinion that such hearings should be open to the press when this is possible without

---

[3] The school authorities in this case not only had information sufficient to form "reasonable cause to believe" plaintiff was using his room in a manner inconsistent with appropriate school discipline, but they also had enough information to amount to probable cause to believe the conduct was criminal.

interference with the orderly operation of the educational institution. But this Court at the same time rules that "an open hearing in the sense that a defendant in a criminal case is entitled to a hearing in open court is not contemplated by the law insofar as the compliance with the procedural rights of students are concerned. . . . The evidence in this case reflects that the school authorities at Troy State University considered it necessary in the exercise of their duty to conduct a relatively closed hearing in order to maintain order and discipline on campus and to avoid interference with the educational function. Any possible prejudice in this case was ameliorated by the fact that plaintiff was given the right to have his counsel attend and the opportunity to confront and fully cross-examine all witnesses against him. In addition, a full transcript of the hearing was made by a court reporter and is a part of the record in this cause.

This Court recognizes that presently in our society, education is no longer a luxury but a necessity. The privilege of attending public educational institutions must be recognized as a right for those qualified to meet the academic requirements and whose conduct does not interfere with the orderly operation of an educational institution. But this does not mean that a disciplinary proceeding held for the purpose of preserving an orderly educational environment through the discipline of those students whose conduct interferes with the educational function is such a proceeding in which all constitutional safeguards are applicable. The Constitution requires only that "rudimentary elements of fair play" be observed and this must be determined on a case-by-case basis. The hearing afforded Moore by Troy State University in this case was in all respects fair and none of Moore's constitutional rights were infringed by reason of the University's action in suspending him.

In accordance with the foregoing, it is the order, judgment and decree of this Court that plaintiff's claim for relief be and is, in each instance, hereby denied. It is ordered that this cause by and the same is hereby dismissed.

It is further ordered that the costs incurred in these proceedings be and the same are hereby taxed against the plaintiff, for which execution may issue.

STUDENTS AND DRUGS

The student personnel officer charged with disciplinary responsibility should try, as much as possible, to treat drug usage by students as an educational problem with legal significance rather than a purely disciplinary problem. One of the most compelling reasons against adopting a purely disciplinary stance on the matter of drug usage is that much of the information which is obtained concerning the use and distribution of drugs and often related dangerous substances generally comes from conversations with students which in many cases are based on interpersonal confidentiality, if not legally privileged confidentiality.

The student personnel officer clearly has certain limitations imposed upon him by law. Nevertheless, he is an educator, and his primary purpose in dealing with student drug users should be to find out why a student is so involved. A recognition of the causative factor in each case can assist the administrator in properly counseling a student and thereby make appropriate legal, psychiatric and medical referrals.

Drug users fall into any number of categories. Nevertheless, three salient student types most often fit the profile of the student drug user: (1) the recreational user, (2) the "pot-lush" or emotionally disoriented individual, and (3) the hard-core abuser who often traffics in drugs.

Although none of these types exist in pure form, the individual administrator should attempt to determine the extent of a student's involvement with drugs and the direction of his usage.

The recreational user consists of those students who are experimenting for the first time or who are weekend social users. They smoke marijuana from time to time and alternately drink beer and wine. Such students are "fun-users" and rarely, if ever, take more dangerous drugs such as LSD or qualudes. Given current social values, there is little more the administrator can do besides discuss the legal and medical implications of a student's behavior, and attempt to help define his degree of risk. Periodic calls by the administrator should be made to ascertain what direction such a student is moving.

The second group represents students who are in a state of emotional disorder. Although few in number, such students constitute a more difficult problem. Most of these students are regular users of marijuana, amphetamines or barbiturates. Many experiment with acid or even cocaine. Drug usage for these students is an everyday practice, and much of their life is drug-centered. They justify their use of drugs on the grounds that it helps them gain insight into themselves and permits them to function more effectively. In actuality such usage is a symptom of a more functional problem, i.e. their inability to cope with and face reality. Fortunately, many of these students will discuss their involvement with drugs. A good number are amenable to professional therapy. Here, the administrator is cautioned not to recommend immediate separation from the college or university. Legal and medical implications should be articulated although they may have little impact on such students.

The hard-core user is the smallest but most difficult group with which to contend. The ideology of this user is highly complicated. He justifies his use of hard drugs on the grounds that he is fully aware of any consequences that may ensue from his usage. He believes he is insulated from legal and medical repercussions. Every probability exists that his use of drugs is suggestive of latent personal problems. Indeed, this individual often sells or distributes drugs as well. He is convinced that drug use is beneficial and that more individuals should participate. Furthermore, his situation may require that he sells drugs in order to support the high cost of his acquired behavior pattern. The administrator in dealing with this individual type should understand that a counseling or educative approach is generally ineffective. The use of hard narcotics by a student is an obvious danger to the welfare of a campus community. Here, the administrator should prudently act to separate this student from campus. Such a student should be permitted to return to campus only after there is medical and psychiatric documentation supporting his rehabilitation.

In working with all of the above types, the administrator should make a distinction between counseling and discipline, i.e. if a student voluntarily admits his usage or involvement with drugs, counseling should have priority over discipline. In those cases where the administrator has received supporting proof of a student's usage or distribution of drugs, and where the student has not voluntarily admitted his usage, discipline has priority over counseling. Here, of course, every effort should be made to protect the student's right to explain and defend his position.

The methodology described above is a practical attempt to make counseling and discipline an extension of a student's educational experience.

Case Study

FACTS ABOUT RON JOHNSON

Ron Johnson is an eighteen-year-old resident freshman at Florham Falls College. Ron's father is a clothier in a nearby town, and together with his wife's part-time teaching salary, the family's income is about $25,000 per year. The Johnsons live in a very attractive home.

During spring vacation, when Ron was helping his father at the clothing store, a student friend, Chuck Thomas, stopped in the store. During the conversation that ensued, Chuck asked Ron if he would like to pool some money, go to Newood and get some "smoke." Ron was somewhat uneasy about the prospect of going to Newood, but his friend assured Ron that he knew of two good contacts in Newood, and that they could purchase enough "smoke" to get Ron that new stereo unit he was talking about at school. When Ron met his school friend in a parking lot at Florham Falls, there was another individual in the car who, according to Chuck Thomas, would be riding along to make sure that everything went off okay. When they reached Newood, they passed a church on Avon Avenue and went down a small street where they stopped. Ron looked around and it was getting a little dark. This looked to him like a pretty rough section of town. As they walked down the small alley toward the auto repair shop where the contact would be made, a tall, strong-looking man appeared out of nowhere and said, "Give me your money." Ron gave the $600 that he had collected from his friends, and then both he and Chuck ran back to the car and left Newood.

On the way back to Florham Falls, everybody talked about how it was "too bad" and how "it was unfortunate that we had to disappoint our friends, but that we were lucky we got out of that one alive." The next day in school, it seems that Ron got pushed around quite a bit by two of his classmates, perhaps because he had neither the "smoke" nor the money they had given him. A residence assistant learned of Ron's difficulty and reported this incident to the dean of students. The dean now has to consider his alternatives.

Problem Analysis

Ron Johnson is a typical middle-class recreational user of drugs, concerned about peer group acceptance. He is young, impulsive and searching for new experiences. Ron has obviously smoked pot before, but is most likely not habituated to its use. Drugs have not become a significant part of his life style.

Ron's experience did not result in any violation of criminal law or campus regulations. Consequently, the dean's approach should emphasize counseling rather than discipline. Since the recreational user is most amenable to understanding the legal and medical risks involved in such behavior, the dean should invite Ron to meet with him in order to discuss the implications of Ron's involvement with drugs and his association with those who attempt to buy and sell drugs. In this particular case, Ron should be urged to make restitution to his friends, perhaps by working off the debt in his father's store. Such restitution will likely reinforce Ron's understanding of responsibility, both for himself and for those with whom he lives. Restitution has the additional benefit of improving Ron's peer relationships.

In this situation, no professional counseling or contact with the police is recommended. The dean, however, should make periodic checks with Ron to see what direction he may be taking.

Subject: A Synthesis and Explanation of Federal Laws Involving Drugs and Controlled Substances

The federal government is presently attempting to update its public health laws just as the various states are doing with regard to the drug abuse problem. New definitions and methods of enforcement are being prepared with the emphasis being placed on an enlightened philosophy with regard to juvenile first offenders. New legislation is being continually proposed. The amount is voluminous. Consequently any presentation of these laws, both new and old, must by necessity be brief, and they must be used only as a first source of guidance. Many, if not most, of these laws are yet untested by the courts and it is unclear what the federal government's ultimate position will be.

There has been, however, a profound recognition that the former body of legislation that controlled such matters was both antiquated and insufficient to meet the needs of present day society. To the end of improving its position in this challenging and often confused body of law, the United States Congress passed the *Comprehensive Drug Abuse Prevention and Control Act of 1970.*

It is the ultimate purpose of this act to provide increased research into and prevention of drug abuse and drug dependence. It also provides for treatment and rehabilitation of drug abusers and drug-dependent persons and attempts to strengthen existing law enforcement authority in the field of drug abuse.

Federal jurisdiction of such controlled substances is obtained because a major portion of the traffic in such substances flows through interstate and foreign commerce. Incidents of the traffic which are not an integral part of such flow, such as manufacture, local distribution and possession, nevertheless have a substantial and direct effect upon interstate commerce. Consequently, as can occur in other areas of federal intervention, it is not exceptionally difficult to establish jurisdiction.

There is a need to understand the present meaning of much terminology used in the federal statutes. Consequently a number of these terms are here defined:

The term "addict" means any individual who habitually uses any *narcotic drug* so as to endanger the public morals, health, safety or welfare, or who is so badly addicted that he has lost the power of self-control with reference to his addiction.

"Controlled substance" means a drug or other substance included in schedules one through five of the Act, part B. The term does not include distilled spirits, wine, malt, beverages or tobacco as those terms are defined in subtitle E of the Internal Revenue Code of 1954.

"Delivery" has been defined as the actual, constructive or *attempted* transfer of a controlled substance whether or not an agency relationship exists. In terms of legal interpretation, the

establishment of an agency relationship can be notoriously difficult; therefore, it has been excluded from the Act. Furthermore,
its relevance here is qustionable.

A point to be emphasized is that the "noxious weed," marijuana,
has been categorized according to its physical structure. Its controlled use includes all parts of the plant Cannabis sativa L,
whether growing or not, including its seeds, resin, compound,
salt, derivative or mixture. *It does not include,* however, the
mature stalks or any compound or derivative except the resin, and
excludes sterilized seeds. There is of course a commercial as well
as chemical reason for the exclusions. A strong rope known as
hemp is made from its stalks, and its seeds (presently sterilized)
is an important ingredient in songbird feed.

The federal definition of the term "narcotic drug," includes
natural or chemically synthesized opium, *coca leaves* and *opiates.*
The term "opiate" means any drug or other substance having
an addiction-forming or addiction-sustaining liability similar to
morphine.

The Attorney General is given the power of enforcement and
may *by rule* add or remove any drug or substance to the schedules
which has a stimulant, depressant or hallucinogenic effect upon
the central nervous system. There are established five schedules of
controlled substances known as Schedules I, II, III, IV and V. The
schedules shall be updated on a semiannual basis initially, and
on an annual basis three years after enactment of this legislation.
Inclusion in the schedules is predicated on the degree of the substance's potential for abuse. Schedule I has the highest, Schedule
V, the lowest. Note that marijuana and its derivatives are included
in Schedule I.

The schedules are listed below along with the penalties for
violation of the acts prohibited. Such acts are the manufacturing,
distributing or possession of a controlled or counterfeit substance.

SCHEDULE I

(a) Unless specifically excepted or unless listed in another schedule, any of the following *opiates,* including their isometers, esters,
ethers, salts and salts of isomers, esters and ethers, whenever the

existence of such isomers, esters, ethers and salts is possible within the specific chemical designation:

(1)	Acetylmethadol	(22)	Etonitazene
(2)	Allylprodine	(23)	Etoxeridine
(3)	Alphacetylmethadol	(24)	Furethidine
(4)	Alphameprodine	(25)	Hydroxpethidine
(5)	Alphamethadol	(26)	Ketobemidone
(6)	Benzethidine	(27)	Levomoramide
(7)	Betacetylmethadol	(28)	Levophenacylmorphan
(8)	Betameprodine	(29)	Morpheridine
(9)	Betamethadol	(30)	Noracymethadol
(10)	Betaprodine	(31)	Norlevorphanol
(11)	Clonitazene	(32)	Normethadone
(12)	Dextromoramide	(33)	Norpipanone
(13)	Dextrorphan	(34)	Phenadoxone
(14)	Diampromide	(35)	Phenampromide
(15)	Diethylthiambutene	(36)	Phenomorphan
(16)	Dimenoxadol	(37)	Phenoperidine
(17)	Dimepheptanol	(38)	Piritramide
(18)	Dimethylthiambutene	(39)	Proheptazine
(19)	Dioxaphetyl butyrate	(40)	Properidine
(20)	Dipipanone	(41)	Racemoramide
(21)	Ethylmethylthiambutene	(42)	Trimeperidine

(b) Unless specifically excepted or unless listed in another schedule, any of the following *opium derivatives,* their salts, isomers and salts of isomers whenever the existence of such salts, isomers and salts of isomers is possible within the specific chemical designation:

(1)	Acetorphine	(12)	Methyldesorphine
(2)	Acetyldihydrocodeine	(13)	Methylhydromorphine
(2)	Benzylmorphine	(14)	Morphine methylbromide
(4)	Codeine methylbromide	(15)	Morphine methylsulfonate
(5)	Codeine-N-Oxide	(16)	Morphine-N-Oxide
(6)	Cyprenorphine	(17)	Myrophine
(7)	Desomorphine	(18)	Nicocodeine
(8)	Dihydromorphine	(19)	Nicomorphine
(9)	Etorphine	(20)	Normorphine
(10)	*Heroin*	(21)	Pholcodine
(11)	Hydromorphinol	(22)	Thebacon

(c) Unless specifically excepted or unless listed in another schedule, any material, compound, mixture or preparation which contains any quantity of the following *hallucinogenic substances,* or which contains any of their salts, isomers and salts of isomers whenever the existence of such salts, isomers and salts of isomers is possible within the specific chemical designation:

    (1) 3,4-methylenedioxy amphetamine
    (2) 5-methoxy-3,4-methylenedioxy amphetamine
    (3) 3,4,5-trimethoxy amphetamine
    (4) Bufotenine
    (5) Diethyltryptamine
    (6) Dimethyltryptamine
    (7) 4-methyl-2,5-dimethoxyamphetamine
    (8) Ibogaine
    (9) Lysergic acid diethylamide
  (10) *Marijuana*
  (11) Mescaline
  (12) Peyote
  (13) N-ethyl-3-piperidyl benzilate
  (14) N-methyl-3-piperidyl benzilate
  (15) Psilocybin
  (16) Psilocyn
  (17) Tetrahydrocannabinols

PENALTY

In the case of a controlled substance in Schedule I or II which is a narcotic drug, such person shall be sentenced to a term of imprisonment of not more than fifteen years, a fine of not more than $25,000, or both. If any person commits such a violation after one or more prior convictions of him for an offense punishable under this paragraph, or for a felony under any other provision of this Title or Title III or other law of the United States relating to narcotic drugs, marijuana, or depressant or stimulant substances, have become final, such person shall be sentenced to a term of imprisonment of not more than thirty years, a fine of not more than $50,000 or both.

Any sentence imposing a term of imprisonment under this paragraph shall, in the absence of such a prior conviction, impose a special parole term of at least three years in addition to such term of imprisonment and shall, if there was such a prior conviction, impose a special parole term of at least six years in addition to such term of imprisonment.

In the case of a *controlled substance* in Schedule I or II which is *not a narcotic* drug or in the case of any *controlled substance in Schedule III,* such person shall be sentenced to a term of imprisonment of not more than five years, a fine of not more than $15,000, or both. If any person commits such a violation after one or more prior convictions of him for an offense punishable under this paragraph, or for a felony under any other provision of this Title, or Title III or other law of the United States relating to narcotic drugs, marijuana or depressant or stimulant substances have become final, such person shall be sentenced to a term of imprisonment of not more than ten years, a fine of not more than $30,000, or both. Any sentence imposing a term of imprisonment under this paragraph shall, in the absence of such a prior conviction, impose a special parole term of at least two years in addition to such term of imprisonment and shall, if there was such a prior conviction, impose a special parole term of at least four years in addition to such term of imprisonment.

SCHEDULE II

(a) Unless specifically excepted or unless listed in another schedule, any of the following substances, whether produced directly or indirectly by extraction from substances of vegetable origin, or independently by means of chemical synthesis, or by a combination of extraction and chemical synthesis:

(1) Opium and opiate, and any salt, compound, derivative or preparation of opium or opiate.

(2) Any salt, compound, derivative or preparation thereof which is chemically equivalent or identical with any of the substances referred to in clause (1), except that these substances shall not include the isoquinoline alkaloids of opium.

(3) Opium poppy and poppy straw.

(4) Coca leaves and any salt, compound, derivative or preparation of coca leaves, and any salt, compound derivative or preparation thereof which is chemically equivalent or identical with any of these substances, except that the substances shall not include decocainized coca leaves or extraction of coca leaves, which extraction do not contain cocaine or ecgonine.

(b) Unless specifically excepted or unless listed in another schedule, any of the following opiates, including their isomers, esters, ethers, salts and salts of isomers, esters and ethers, whenever the existence of such isomers, esters, ethers and salts is possible within the specific chemical designation:

(1) Alphaprodine
(2) Anileridine
(3) Bezitramide
(4) Dihydrocodeine
(5) Diphenoxylate
(6) Fentanyl
(7) Isomethadone
(8) Levomethorphan
(9) Levorphanol
(10) Metazocine
(11) Methadone
(12) Methadone-Intermediate, 4-cyano-2-dimethyl-amino-4,4-diphenyl butane
(13) Moramide-Intermediate, 2-methyl-3-morpholino-1, 1-diphenylpropane-carboxylic acid
(14) Pethidine
(15) Pethidine-Intermediate-A, 4-cyano-1-methyl-4-phenylpiperidine
(16) Pethidine-Intermediate-B, ethyl-4-phenylpiperidine-4-carboxylice
(17) Pethidine-Intermediate-C, 1-methyl-4-phenylpiperidine-4-carboxylic acid
(18) Phenazocine
(19) Piminodine
(20) Racemethorphan
(21) Racemorphan

(c) Unless specifically excepted or unless listed in another schedule, any injectable liquid which contains any quantity of methamphetamine, including its salts, isomers and salts of isomers.

PENALTY

In the case of a controlled substance in Schedule I or II which is a *narcotic drug,* such person shall be sentenced to a term of imprisonment of not more than fifteen years, a fine of not more than $25,000, or both. If any person commits such a violation after one or more prior convictions of him for an offense punishable under this paragraph, or for a felony under any other provision of this Title or Title III or other law of the United States relating to narcotic drugs, marijuana or depressant or stimulant substances, have become final, such person shall be sentenced to a term of imprisonment of not more than thirty years, a fine of not more than $50,000, or both.

Special Parole Term

Any sentence imposing a term of imprisonment under this paragraph shall, in the absence of such a prior conviction, impose a special parole term of at least three years in addition to such term of imprisonment and shall, if there was such a prior conviction, impose a special parole term of at least six years in addition to such term of imprisonment.

In the case of a controlled substance in Schedule I or II which is not a narcotic drug or in the case of any controlled substance in Schedule III, such person shall be sentenced to a term of imprisonment of not more than five years, a fine of not more than $15,000, or both. If any person commits such a violation after one or more prior convictions of him for an offense punishable under this paragraph, or for a felony under any other provision of this Title or Title III or other law of the United States relating to narcotic drugs, marijuana or depressant or stimulant substances, have become final, such person shall be sentenced to a term of imprisonment of not more than ten years, a fine of not more than $30,000, or both. Any sentence imposing a term of imprisonment under this paragraph shall, in the absence of such a prior conviction, impose a special parole term of at least two years in addition to such term of imprisonment and shall, if there was such a prior conviction, impose a special parole term of at least four years in addition to such term of imprisonment.

SCHEDULE III

    (a) Unless specifically excepted or unless listed in another schedule, any material, compound, mixture or preparation which contains any quantity of the following substances having a *stimulant effect* on the central nevvous system:

        (1) Amphetamine, its salts, optical isomers and salts of its optical isomers

        (2) Phenmetrazine and its salts

        (3) Any substance (except in injectable liquid) which contains

any quantity of methamphetamine, including its salts, isomers and salts of isomers

    (4) Methylphenidate

(b) Unless specifically excepted or unless listed in another schedule, any material, compound, mixture or preparation which contains any quantity of the following substances having a *depressant effect* on the central nervous system:

    (1) Any substance which contains any quantity of a derivative of barbituric acid or any salt of a derivative of barbituric acid

    (2) Chorhexadol

    (3) Gluthethimide

    (4) Lysergic acid

    (5) Lysergic acid amide

    (6) Methyprylon

    (7) Phencyclidine

    (8) Sulfondiethylmethane

    (9) Sulfonethylmethane

    (10) Sulfonmethane

(c) Nalorphine

(d) Unless specifically excepted or unless listed in another schedule, any material, compound, mixture, or preparation containing limited quantities or any of the following narcotic drugs, or any salts thereof:

    (1) Not more than 1.8 grams of codeine per one hundred milliliters or not more than ninety milligrams per dosage unit with an equal or greater quantity of an isoquinoline alkaloid of opium

    (2) Not more than 1.8 grams of codeine per one hundred milliliters or not more than ninety milligrams per dosage unit, with one or more active, non-narcotic ingredients in recognized therapeutic amounts

    (3) Not more than 300 milligrams of dihydrocodeinone per one hundred milliliters or not more than fifteen milligrams per dosage unit, with a four-fold or greater quantity of an isoquinoline alkaloid of opium

    (4) Not more than 300 milligrams of dihydrocodeinone per one hundred milliliters or not more than fifteen milligrams per dosage unit, with one or more active, non-narcotic ingredients in recognized therapeutic amounts

    (5) Not more than 1.8 grams of dihydrocodeine per one hundred milliliters or not more than ninety milligrams per dosage unit, with one or more active, non-narcotic ingredients in recognized therapeutic amounts

(6) Not more than 300 milligrams of ethylmorphine per one hundred milliliters or not more than fifteen milligrams per dosage unit, with one or more active, non-narcotic ingredients in recognized therapeutic amounts

(7) Not more than 500 milligrams of opium per one hundred milliliters or per one hundred grams, or not more than twenty-five milligrams per dosage unit, with one or more active, non-narcotic ingredients in recognized therapeutic amounts

(8) Not more than fifty milligrams of morphine per one hundred grams with one or more active, non-narcotic ingredients in recognized therapeutic amounts

PENALTY

In the case of a controlled substance in Schedule I or II which is not a narcotic drug or in the case of any controlled substance in Schedule III, such person shall be sentenced to a term of imprisonment of not more than five years, a fine of not more than $15,000, or both. If any person commits such a violation after one or more prior convictions of him for an offense punishable under this paragraph, or for a felony under any other provision of this Title or Title III or other law of the United States relating to narcotic drugs, marijuana or depressant or stimulant substances have become final, such person shall be sentenced to a term of imprisonment of not more than ten years, a fine of not more than $30,000, or both. Any sentence imposing a term of imprisonment under this paragraph shall, in the absence of such a prior conviction, impose a special parole term of at least two years in addition to such term of imprisonment and shall, if there was such a prior conviction, impose a special parole term of at least four years in addition to such term of imprisonment.

Schedule IV

(1) Barbital
(2) Chloral betaine
(3) Chloral hydrate
(4) Ethchlorvynol
(5) Ethinamate
(6) Methohexital
(7) Meprobamate
(8) Methylphenobarbital
(9) Paraldehyde
(10) Petrichloral
(11) Phenobarbital

PENALTY

In the case of a controlled substance in Schedule IV, such person shall be sentenced to a term of imprisonment of not more than three years, a fine of not more than $10,000, or both. If any person commits such a violation after one or more prior convictions of him for an offense punishable under this paragraph, or for a felony under any other provision of this Title or Title III or other law of the United States relating to narcotic drugs, marijuana or depressant or stimulant substances have become final, such person shall be sentenced to a term of imprisonment of not more than six years, a fine of not more than $20,000, or both. Any sentence imposing a term of imprisonment under this paragraph shall, in the absence of such a prior conviction, impose a special parole term of at least one year in addition to such term of imprisonment and shall, if there was such a prior conviction, impose a special parole term of at least two years in addition to such term of imprisonment.

SCHEDULE V

Any compound, mixture or preparation containing any of the following limited quantities of narcotic drugs, which shall include one or more non-narcotic active medicinal ingredients in sufficient proportion to confer upon the compound, mixture or preparation valuable medicinal qualities other than those possessed by the narcotic drug alone:

(1) Not more than 200 milligrams of codeine per one hundred milliliters or per one hundred grams.
(2) Not more than one hundred milligrams of dihydrocodeine per one hundred milliliters or per one hundred grams.
(3) Not more than one hundred milligrams of ethylmorphine per one hundred milliliters or per one hundred grams.
(4) Not more than 2.5 milligrams of diphenoxylate
(5) Not more than one hundred milligrams of opium per one hundred milliliters or per one hundred grams.

The Attorney General may by regulation except any compound, mixture or preparation containing any depressant or stimulant substance in paragraph (a) or (b) of Schedule III or in Schedule IV or V from the application of all or any part of this Title if (1) the compound, mixture or preparation contains one or more active medicinal ingredients not having a depressant or stimulant effect on the central nervous system, and (2) such ingredients are included therein in such combinations, quantity, proportion or concentration as to vitiate the potential for abuse of the substances which do have a depressant or stimulant effect on the central nervous system.

PENALTY

In the case of a controlled substance in Schedule V, such person shall be sentenced to a term of imprisonment of not more than one year, a fine of not more than $5,000, or both. If any person commits such a violation after one or more convictions of him for an offense punishable under this paragraph, or for a crime under any other provision of this Title or Title III or other law of the United States relating to narcotic drugs, marijuana or depressant stimulant substances have become final, such person shall be sentenced to a term of imprisonment of not more than two years, a fine of not more than $10,000, or both. It is further stipulated that any person who distributes any amount of marijuana for *no remuneration* shall be treated as violating the rules for *simple possession* of a controlled substance and sentenced to a term of imprisonment of not more than one year, a fine of not more than $5,000, or both. The penalties are doubled for previous offenders. All special parole terms may be revoked if its terms and conditions are violated.

There has been a *significant change in the area of simple possession* of narcotic drug and controlled substances. In such cases where possession was not obtained through a valid prescription or order from a licensed practitioner the violator shall be sentenced to a term of imprisonment of not more than one year, a fine of not more than $5,000, or both. The penalties are doubled for previous offenders.

Where a person is convicted of a first offense of simple possession the court may, without entering a judgment of guilty, and with the consent of such person, place him on probation for a period not to exceed one year. If during the period of probation the person does not violate his probation the proceedings may, in the courts' discretion be dismissed and the probation ended.

If the period of probation is not violated, at its conclusion, the court shall dismiss the proceedings and the person discharged.

Upon the dismissal of such person and discharge of the proceedings against him, an application may be made to the court that *all official records be expunged.* This is only possible if the person was not over the age of twenty-one at the time of the offense.

The federal government has seen fit to create another category in addition to those aforementioned, that is one of distribution to persons under the age of twenty-one years. In such cases, if the person is at least eighteen years of age and a *first offender* he may be punished by a term of imprisonment of ten years, a fine of not more than $30,000, or both. A special parole term of at least four years is also imposed. Any person at least eighteen years of age who is a *previous offender* may be punished by a term of imprisonment of up to fifteen years, a fine up to $45,000, or both. A special parole term of at least eighteen years is also imposed.

Any person who attempts or conspires to commit any offense as previously defined is punishable by imprisonment or fine or both which may not exceed the maximum punishment prescribed for the offense, the commission of which was the object of the attempt or conspiracy.

All penalties imposed are in addition to and not in lieu of any civil or administrative penalties or sanctions authorized by law. Any penalties for violation of state criminal or civil laws shall also be in addition to the above insofar as there is no violation of the double jeopardy provisions of federal and state law.

A liberal and extremely controversial policy to break and enter under certain conditions is also permitted by officers or employees of the Attorney General.

Where a United States Judge or Magistrate issued a search warrant, satisfied that a probable cause exists, any officer authorized to execute a search warrant may without notice of his authority or purpose break open an outer or inner door or window of a building where the giving of notice may endanger his life or the property being sought may be quickly destroyed or dispensed of.

For the purpose of these actions, the term "probable cause" means a valid public interest in the effective enforcement of these laws sufficient to justify administrative inspections under the circumstances specified in the application for the warrant.

In conclusion it must be stated that although the federal attempt to control drug abuse is quite comprehensive and utilizes a modern socio-legal approach to this highly troubled area of social involvement, laws are only a tool in an attempt to control illicit manufacture, distribution and utilization of these addictive substances.

The drug problem goes deeper than mere widespread use of these materials. It is in part derived from the physiological and mental make up of a people, which undeniably is an important factor in the development of addiction, but it is substantially aggravated by a general weakening of a culture's social and moral fabric.

It is strongly recommended that in all cases in which this memorandum is utilized that other appropriate medical, legal and other relevant consultations be made.

CHAPTER V

Students, Civil Liberties, and the Law

G IVEN THE INCREASING NUMBER of students who have reached adult status, either through legislation or judicial decision, the rights and responsibilities of students are not as distinguishable from other members of the campus community as they once were. The fact that adult status has been conferred upon most students is suggestive of their increased participation in the growth and direction of the institution they attend. Although there is no legal right to such participation, prudent university officials will increasingly consult with student groups. Indeed, many university students, having been enfranchised, vote in public elections and may even become elected officials. Student status, in and of itself, does not confer upon the individual greater prerogatives than he otherwise would have, but certainly no less because of it.

Freedom of speech, freedom of association, the right to privacy and the confidentiality of student records, however, have special meaning to the student and the college administrator, and accordingly become areas of concern.

Freedom of Speech

The student personnel administrator is most likely to face questions of free speech in the context of student dissent. Freedom of expression should be regarded as a matter of right in any educational institution. Students have the right to speak, and to publish without prior administrative approval. To be sure, such speech or publication should not interrupt the normal operation of the college or university, and also should fall within the law against slander and libel. Students, of course, may criticize their institution and this prerogative has considerable support in the law. The dean of students should recognize that student dissent, whether it be expressed in campus newspapers or in rallies, is often, although not always, a function of administrative policy which previously has excluded meaningful student participation.

Freedom of Association

Students are generally free to organize and to join associations. It has recently been declared by the Supreme Court that a university cannot arbitrarily proscribe clubs or associations from campus. For those clubs that request funds from the university, it is doubtless necessary to take reasonable precautions to prevent the misallocation of monies collected for the general welfare of the student body. Organizations should not be required, however, to submit membership lists. Such lists, when they exist, should not be freely distributed, except for the limited purpose of investigation of alleged improper use of funds.

Given the student's right to organize and join associations, he also has the concomitant right to utilize campus facilities under the following circumstances.

(1) An association may not infringe upon the rights of others.
(2) An association may not discriminate on the basis of race, sex or creed. It may not misuse student funds or facilities for activities which may violate relevant IRS statues or other relevant municipal, state or federal law.

The university, of course, may demand that every organization identify an individual who serves as a representative of a student organization and who is responsible for communications with the institution.

Right to Privacy

All duly registered students should be given the right to live and work as they please so long as the health and safety of other campus citizens is not endangered. When civil officials intrude on the privacy of the student, they should do so with the understanding that the private quarters of the student are protected by relevant constitutional guarantees. The standards and procedures for civil intrusion should be no less stringent than would normally be accepted in private homes outside the campus. Academic and personal records of a student's progress should be kept separate in order to minimize disclosures that may be damaging to a student's reputation and employability. Disciplinary or counseling files should not be generally available to unauthorized persons, whether they be within the institution or outside the institution without written consent of the student involved.

MODEL UNIVERSITY AND CAMPUS POLICIES

These materials consist of selected university policies and rules and have been arranged under the following subject heads:

(1) Charter to the Student Communities
(2) Statement on Student Rights and Welfare
(3) Campus Rules
(4) Constitution of the Campus Tribunal

These policies and procedures are included as an illustration of the broad range of a campus disciplinary system. These rules are not summarized or abstracted so school administrators or student governing bodies may find specific guidelines for their assistance.

CHARTER TO THE STUDENT COMMUNITY OF THE UNIVERSITY

The Trustees of the University dedicated to the perpetuation of a democratic society and convinced of the value of student self-government do hereby grant this charter to the student communities of the University. In so doing, the Trustees of the University not only recognize the responsibilities of student government, but also take note of the concomitant administrative, legal and financial responsibilities of the University. This is particularly true regarding the University responsibility for student activities fees, which are collected by the University. The University cannot avoid its responsibilities in the collection and disbursement of these monies; and, therefore, must share with students these responsibilities.

Through a process of shared responsibility, it is expected that the underlying goals of collegiality can be attained.

ARTICLE I

Authority for the creation of student governments is herewith vested in the student communities. This authority is to be exercised in the following areas:

Section 1

To adopt a constitution for the democratic regulation of certain student affairs as hereinafter set forth. The constitution so adopted must be in accord with the provisions of this charter and the amendments thereto as added from time to time.

Section 2

To elect a representative student government and student officers for the purpose of deliberation upon and administering the affairs of the student community in keeping with the powers and privileges bestowed by this charter.

ARTICLE II

The student governments shall have the power and duty:

Section 1

To advise the University community of the needs and interests of the student communities and to work constantly to assure capable students representation on all campus and university organizations and committees dealing especially with the needs and interests of students. Specifically, the student governments shall:

(1) Maintain liaison with the administration for information concerning University policy.
(2) Participate with other student organizations in the establishment and allocation of activities fees for the maintenance of the student activities program.
(3) Plan and execute intellectual, citizenship and social programs of the student communities.
(4) Charter those organizations of the student communities related to the functions of the student governments in accordance with University regulations.
(5) Provide for participation in the discussion of any matter of concern to the student communities through the appropriate bodies, such as the campus councils and the University Senate.

Section 2
Enabling By-Laws

To recognize its responsibility in connection with the preceding section, to carry out these obligations, the student governments shall:

Maintain liaison with the University community by inviting campus-administrators and faculty to attend student government meetings.
Establish qualifications of student office within their constitutions.

Obtain the approval of the Dean of Students or his designate for any event held under University sponsorship.

Under the advisorship of the Dean of Students or his designate plan and execute all of the student programming for which it is responsible.

Through meetings with all the student organizations involved and with the appropriate campus and University officials make recommendations upon the level of the activities fee on each campus. No charge of fees shall become effective without the approval of the student body by referendum.

Submit to the Dean of Students or his designate at an appropriate time during each fiscal year an anticipated budget for the year.

Assume no financial obligations until the budget has been approved by the Dean of Students or his designate, and to secure his approval before incurring any expenditure.

STATEMENT ON STUDENT RIGHTS AND WELFARE

I. Freedom of Access

The admissions policies of the University should clearly state the characteristics of students and the expectations of the University which are relevant to success in the institution's program. The University shall be open to all students who are qualified according to its admission standards.

The facilities and services of the University shall be open to all enrolled students, and the institution shall use its influence to secure, for all students, equal access to public facilities in the local community.

II. In the Classroom

Instructors should encourage free discussion, inquiry and expression. Student performance should be evaluated solely on an academic basis, not on the basis of opinions or conduct unrelated to academic standards.

A. Protection of Freedom of Expression: Students are free to take reasoned exception to information or views offered in any course of study and to reserve judgment about matters of opinion. They are, however, responsible for learning the content of any course of study in which they are enrolled. The instructor is responsible for presenting appropriate content in any course he or she undertakes to teach.

B. Protection Against Improper Academic Evaluation: Students are protected through established procedures against prejudiced or capricious academic evaluation. At the same time, they are responsible for maintaining standards of academic performance established for each course in which they are enrolled.

C. Protection Against Improper Disclosure: Information on student views, beliefs and political associations which instructors may acquire in the course of their work as teachers, advisors and counselors is considered confidential.

D. Attendance: Students have the right to the full attention of qualified instructors for a prescribed number of class hours in each course of study. Students are responsible for taking full advantage of the opportunities and conditions provided in the classroom.

III. Student Records

In order to minimize the risk of improper disclosure, academic and nonacademic records are maintained separately, and access to each is regulated by explicit policies established on each of the University's campuses.

Transcripts of academic records contain academic information only. Information from nonacademic records such as disciplinary or counseling files is not available to persons not specifically authorized by the above-mentioned policies without the express consent of the student involved, except under legal compulsion or in cases where the safety of persons not specifically authorized by the above-mentioned policies without the express consent of the student involved, except under legal compulsion or in cases where the safety of persons or property is threatened. Official permanent records do not reflect the political activities or beliefs of students.

IV. Advisory and Counseling Services

In order to assist and support the student's academic growth and personal development, the following services are provided:

A. Academic Advising and Counseling:

1. An academic advisory system providing guidance for planning programs and schedules, reviewing progress, advice on graduate and professional school and assistance in obtaining admission to such schools when appropriate.

2. An academic counseling service assisting students experiencing academic difficulty and providing professional guidance in assessing the nature of their problems, and in developing skills necessary for success in their college programs.

B. Personal Counseling:

1. A personal counseling service providing professional guidance to students having vocational or psychological problems, and a referral service for those requiring therapy.

2. Religious organizations establishing and maintaining counseling services for the University's student body.

C. Health Service: The University health service providing first aid services.

D. Financial Aid: Campus financial aid offices providing information on and procedures for the acquisition of scholarships, academic loans and other programs of student aid.

E. Placement Service: Campus student placement services assisting undergraduates and graduates in locating employment opportunities, and providing information on career opportunities.

Students are responsible for securing the assistance provided by these services whenever a need appears or when a counselor or faculty member recommends them.

V. Student Participation in Institutional Government

As constituents of the University academic community, students are free, individually and collectively, to express their interest to the student body.

In order to give effect to this principle, provision has been made for student representations on the Board of Trustees, in the University Senate, on the Campus Councils, on College and Departmental Committees and a number of other decision-making and deliberating bodies.

VI. Disciplinary Standards and Procedures

At the University, disciplinary procedures are substantially secondary to the use of example, counseling, guidance and admonition in the maintenance of responsible student conduct.

The University, however, has the duty and corollary disciplinary power to protect its educational purpose through the setting of standards of students' scholarship and student conduct and through the regulation of the use of institutional facilities. In the exceptional circumstances, when the preferred means fail to resolve problems of student conduct, procedural safeguards protect the student from unfair imposition of serious penalties.

A. Standards of Conduct Expected of Students: The University campus establishes and makes known standards of behavior which it considers essential to its educational mission and campus life. Such general behavioral expectations, the resultant specific regulations and disciplinary procedures have been formulated with student participation and are published in the campus student handbook or in other equally available publications.

B. Investigation of Student Conduct:

1. Premises occupied by students and personal possessions of students shall be searched only when a warrant authorized by law is produced or if permission of the occupant has been given and in the presence of the occupant, except under circumstances believed to be a threat to life and safety.

2. Students detected or arrested in the course of serious violations of institutional regulations, or infractions of ordinary law, shall be informed of their rights. No form of harassment shall be used by institutional representatives to coerce admissions of guilt or to obtain information on the activities of other suspected persons.

C. Status of Student Pending Final Action: Pending action on charges, the status of an accused student is not altered, and his right to be present on the campus and to attend classes is maintained, except when the student's safety and well-being or that of the University community is judged to be in jeopardy.

D. Hearing Committee: When a student is charged with a misconduct and chooses not to accept Dean of Student's discipline, or if the student questions the fairness of disciplinary action to be taken against him, he is granted, on request, the privilege of a hearing before a regularly-constituted campus hearing committee authorized by the Campus Council.

VII. Off-Campus Freedom of Students

A. Exercise of Rights of Citizenship: University students are both citizens and members of the academic community. As citizens, students enjoy the same freedom of speech, peaceful assembly, the rights of petition that other citizens enjoy and, as members of the academic community, they are subject to the obligations which accrue to them by virtue of this membership. Faculty members and administrative officials shall insure that institutional powers are not employed to inhibit such intellectual and personal development of students as is often promoted by their exercise of rights of citizenship both on and off campus.

B. Institutional Authority and Civil Penalties: Activities of students may upon occasion result in violation of law. In such cases, institutional officials are prepared to apprise students of sources of legal counsel and may offer other assistance. Students who violate the law may incur penalties prescribed by civil authorities, but institutional authority shall never be used merely to duplicate the function of general laws. Only where the institution's interests as an academic community are distinctly and clearly involved shall the special authority of the institution be asserted. The student who incidently violates institutional regulations in the course of his off-campus activity, shall be subject to no greater penalty than is normally imposed. Institutional action shall always be independent of community pressure.

VIII. Student Affairs: Life and Welfare

A. Student Government: The role of the student government at the University, and both the general and specific responsibilities is set forth in University Canon, and the actions of student government within its jurisdiction may be reviewed only through orderly and prescribed procedures.

B. Freedom of Association: Students bring to the campuses a variety of interests as members of the academic community. They are free to organize and join associations to promote their common interests.

1. The membership, policies and actions of a student organization shall be determined by vote of only those persons who hold bona fide membership in the college, campus or University community.

2. Institutional recognition of a student organization shall not be withheld solely on grounds of its affiliation with an extramural organization.

3. Each student organization, if they elect to, shall be free to choose its own campus advisor who may advise organizations in the exercise of responsibility, but who shall not have the authority to control such organizations.

4. Student organizations may be required to submit a statement of purpose, criteria for membership, rules of procedures and a current list of officers. They shall not be required to submit a membership list as a condition of institutional recognition.

5. Campus organizations, including those affiliated with an extramural organization, shall be open to all students genuinely interested in the objectives of the organization.

C. Freedom of Inquiry and Expression:

Students and student organizations are free to examine and to discuss all questions of interest to them, and to express opinions publicly and privately. They are free to support causes by orderly means which do not disrupt the regular and essential operation of the institution. At the same time, it should be made clear to the academic and the larger community that, in their public expressions or demonstrations, students or student organizations speak only for themselves.

2. Students may invite and hear any person of their own choosing. Routine procedures required in relation to guest speakers on campus shall be designed only to insure orderly scheduling of facilities and adequate preparation for the event, and that the occasion is conducted in a manner appropriate to an academic community. The institutional control of campus facilities shall not be used as a device of censorship. Sponsorship of guest speakers does not imply approval or endorsement of the views expressed, either by the sponsoring group or the institution.

D. Student Publications: Student publications and the student press are valuable aids in establishing and maintaining an atmosphere of free and responsible discussion and of intellectual exploration on the campus. They are media for bringing student concerns to the attention of the faculty and institutional authorities, and for formulating student opinion on various issues on the campus and in the world at large.

It is the policy of the University to encourage and promote the development of student newspapers published by independent corporations financially and legally separate from the University. Until such financial and legal autonomy is finally possible, the University, as publisher of student publications, may have to bear the legal responsibility for their content.

The editorial freedom of student editors and managers entails corollary responsibilities to be governed by the canons of responsible journalism, such as the avoidance of libel, indecency, undocumented allegations, attacks on personal integrity and the techniques of harassment and innuendo. As safeguards for the editorial freedom of student publications, the following provisions are necessary:

1. The student press shall be free of censorship and advance approval of copy, and its editors and managers shall be free to develop their own editorial policies and news coverage.

2. Editors and managers of student publications shall be protected from arbitrary suspension and removal because of student, faculty, administrative or public disapproval of editorial policy or content. Only for proper and stated causes shall editors and managers be subject to removal, and then by orderly and prescribed procedures. The campus agency responsible for the appointment of editors and managers shall be the agency responsible for their removal.

3. All University published and financed student publications shall

explicitly state on the editorial page that the opinions therein expressed are not necessarily those of the University, or of the student body.

The above model charter was prepared, after consultation with the authors, by a Fairleigh Dickinson University committee on Student Rights and Welfare, chaired by Mr. David Watson of the University's Office of Institutional Studies. It is an adaptation and expansion of the Joint Statement on Rights and Freedoms of Students originally drafted in 1967 by representatives from the American Association of University Professors, U. S. National Student Association, Association of American Colleges, National Association of Student Personnel Administrators and National Association of Women Deans and Counselors.

CAMPUS REGULATIONS

Alcoholic Beverages

The consumption of alcoholic beverages at student functions clearly has the potential of violating relevant state statutes. Divisions of Alcoholic Beverage Control have promulgated statements of policy concerning the distribution of alcoholic beverages to students under the age of majority.

Student groups wishing to have alcoholic beverages available at their function should meet the following specifications:

1. A social function must be private, i.e. it must be sponsored by a specific group and be open only to members and guests.
2. Beverages must be purchased from the funds of a general treasury.
3. If admission charges are made for a social function, alcoholic beverages cannot be served as part of the admission price.
4. If alcoholic beverages are served at a social event, the sponsoring group must identify an individual of legal age who will assume responsibility for the purchase of such beverages and the conduct of attending members and guests.

Student groups which fail to meet the above specifications will be subject to the loss of campus privileges and funding.

A legal memorandum concerning consumption of alcohol has been prepared by Student Personnel Legal Counselor, Professor Joseph Tramutola. It is available in the Dean of Students' Office, on request, for further clarification.

Campus Pets

Effective January 28, 1972, the Campus Policy for all members of the campus community is that no pets are allowed on campus. The only exception will be duly registered seeing-eye dogs.

Students who violate the policy will be subject to the due process established by the Dean of Students. Faculty and staff who violate the policy will be subject to a due process to be established by the Campus Provost.

Campus Drug Policy

The use of drugs without a medical prescription is illegal. Individuals who sell or distribute drugs are subject to state and federal criminal law. Individuals who either sell or transfer drugs of any kind are subject to campus disciplinary action and can be separated from the University. Individuals who use drugs are subject to campus disciplinary action except when they voluntarily seek and continue university counseling assistance.

University personnel, however, cannot legally protect individuals who have drug emergencies, but they can secure medical help through our Campus Health Service.

N. B. Our Campus Health Service is required by law to send all individuals with drug overdoses to local hospital emergency rooms. Despite possible legal consequences, responsible action should be taken to prevent injury or death.

Political Activities

No duly constituted group which is supported in any way by the University may sponsor programs or participate in behalf of any political candidate.

All facilities and services other than those assigned for purposes of distributing literature or public speaking shall be paid for according to appropriate campus rates. No undue length of time should be allotted to any one political group.

No staff or faculty member shall contribute services during the period of time for which he is being compensated by the University.

Any class which is formally scheduled should not participate directly or indirectly in any activity which a political organization may sponsor on campus except for auditing purposes.

American Council on Education Guidelines,
June 21, 1970, Code Sec. 501 (c) (3)

Educational institutions traditionally have recognized and provided facilities on an impartial basis to various activities on the college campuses, even those activities which have a partisan political bent, such as for example, the Republican, Democratic and other political clubs. This presents no problem. However, to the extent that such organizations extend their activities beyond the campus, and intervene or participate in campaigns on behalf of candidates for public office, or permit nonmembers of the university community to avail themselves of university facilities or services, an institution should in good faith make certain that proper and appropriate charges are made and collected for all facilities and services provided. Extraordinary or prolonged use of facilities, particularly by nonmembers of the university community, even with reimbursement, might raise questions. Such organizations should be prohibited from soliciting in the name of the University funds to be used in such off-campus intervention or participation.

Guidelines Regarding Dissent

The academic community of the University shall be preserved as a free and open society with all campus community citizens encouraged to speak freely, to protest, to organize, to demonstrate, to dissent from any decision on any issue and to demonstrate the dissent by any orderly means. Assemblages and activities that obstruct or disrupt teaching, research, administration or other University activities are considered to be unacceptable.

1. Every campus citizen wishing to register his dissent is encouraged to do so through established campus channels available to every member of the University community. Students who wish to demonstrate must file the necessary event forms available in the Student Activities Office to reserve the appropriate time and facility, whether indoors or outdoors. Faculty and staff who wish to demonstrate must similarly comply by submitting requests to the Office of Special Programs and Public Affairs.
2. Students, faculty and staff who are demonstrating are required to avoid academic and administrative buildings during their demonstration so that there is no obstruction or disruption of the teaching, research, administrative or other University activity. Any obstructive or disruptive activity that presents a clear and present danger to the freedom and openness of the campus community will be dealt with internally as a serious matter with penalties.
3. Any penalties assessed as a result of violation of freedom and openness of the campus community shall be imposed according to due process.
4. Failure to comply with internal decisions to end disruptive or obstruc-

JUDICIAL PROCESS FLOW CHART

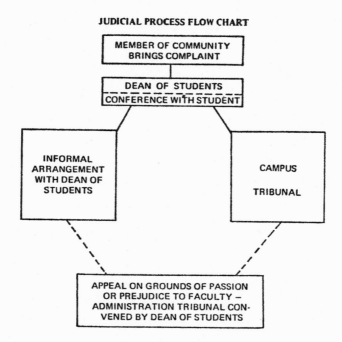

tive activities may require off-campus assistance and subject those participating to arrest.

5. Nonmembers of the campus community involved in disruptions or obstructive activities will be dealt with by off-campus authorities.

Procedure

Members of the Campus Community, whether as individuals or groups, are expected to obey all federal, state and local laws.

The campus judicial system permits members of the community to register any complaints against individuals or groups with the Dean of Students. Complaints may come from students, faculty, deans, counselors or any interested individuals. If the complaint warrants adjudication, the Dean of Students will summon the accused and discuss with him disciplinary procedures and options that may be available.

The accused may elect to accept an informal disciplinary arrangement with the Dean of Students or may request a hearing before the Campus Tribunal. Appeal on grounds of passion or prejudice is available through the Dean of Students' Office.

CONSTITUTION OF THE CAMPUS TRIBUNAL

ARTICLE I

NAME AND PURPOSE

Section 1—The name of this organization will be the Campus Tribunal of the University.

Section 2—This organization will be concerned with disciplinary actions pertaining to students and advisory resolutions concerning student life and welfare.

ARTICLE II

MEMBERSHIP

Section 1—The Tribunal will have four student members and one alternate student member.

    A. The alternate student member will only have a vote if any member of the Tribunal is absent.

Section 2—One faculty member nominated by the faculty will serve as a judge with full voting rights.

    A. One faculty member nominated by the faculty will act as an advisor and an alternate to the faculty judge.

Section 3—A voting chairman will be selected from among the student members of the Tribunal.

ARTICLE III

QUALIFICATIONS

Section 1—Any full-time student of the University may be a member of the Tribunal if he meets the qualifications.

Section 2—A student on disciplinary probation at the time of appointment is not eligible to be on the Tribunal. A student who goes on disciplinary probation may not maintain his office.

Section 3—No member of the Student Senate may be a member of the Campus Tribunal.

ARTICLE IV

APPOINTMENTS

Section 1—The members of the Tribunal will be appointed each spring by the newly elected Student Senate.

    A. The members of the Senate may nominate students for the Tribunal.
    B. The nominations will be sent to a committee of Senators who will give their recommendations to the entire Senate.
    C. The Senate will then vote on the committee's recommendations.

D. If the Senate does not approve any recommendation of the committee, the floor will then be open for any new nomination to the Tribunal.
E. In case of a tie between four and five and/or five and six, the Senate president will break the tie.
F. All appointments are for a one-year term.
G. The Senate will appoint a new judge or alternate in case of a permanent vacancy.

ARTICLE V

JURISDICTION

Section 1—The campus judicial system permits members of the community to register any complaints against individuals or groups with the Dean of Students. Complaints may come from students, faculty, deans, counselors or any interested individuals. If the complaint warrants adjudication, the Dean of Students will summon the accused and discuss with him disciplinary procedures and options that may be available. The accused may elect to accept an informal disciplinary arrangement with the Dean of Students or may request a hearing before the Campus Tribunal. Appeal on grounds of passion or prejudice is available through the Dean of Students' Office.

Section 2—Judicial Process Flow Chart

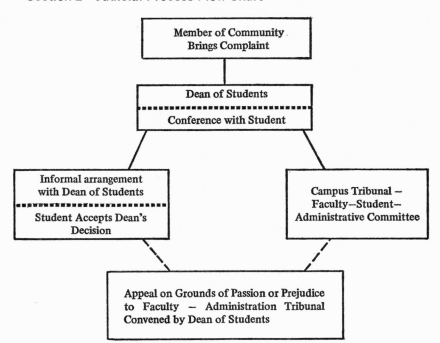

ARTICLE VI

PROCEDURES

Section 1—Any student who elects to appear before the Campus Tribunal is bound by its verdict unless he wishes to appeal the decision.

Section 2—If a student wishes to present a case to the Tribunal, he must obtain a petition for a hearing at the Dean of Students' Office and return the petition to the same office.

A. All petitions must be answered as to whether or not the Tribunal will hear the case and returned to the student within three school days unless there are extenuating circumstances making this impossible.
B. If the petition is rejected, the reasons for the rejection must be clearly stated.

Section 3—The Tribunal must hear the case within one school week after the acceptance of the petition unless there are extenuating circumstances making this impossible.

Section 4—There must be 100 percent quorum at all hearings.

Section 5—The Tribunal will prepare its own procedure for the hearings which will be conducted by its Chairman.

Section 6—All decisions of the Tribunal will be by majority vote.

Section 7—All decisions of punishment to the student must be waived pending the findings of the Tribunal, except in extraordinary circumstances as determined by the Dean of Students.

Section 8—If a student, or his authorized representative, does not appear for the case and does not, in the opinion of the Tribunal, give adequate reasons, the Tribunal may treat his case in the manner it believes just.

Section 9—A hearing may be closed to the public upon the request of the student or the Tribunal.

Section 10—In cases that require penalties, the Campus Tribunal will decide what sanctions are necessary and have the power to impose them through the Office of the Dean of Students.

Section 11—Any judge may remove himself from a case if he feels there is a conflict of interest.

Section 12—In cases where it is impossible to have the 100 percent quorum through normal channels, the chairman may appoint a temporary judge for that case with majority consent of the Tribunal.

ARTICLE VII
REMOVAL PROCEDURES

Section 1—Any student member of the Tribunal may be removed from office by the Senate for reasons of nonfulfillment of duties essential to the office or for behavior which is not becoming to a member. A full hearing must be held with all parties concerned being present. A three-quarters majority of the voting members present is required.

ARTICLE VIII

Section 1—Any amendment to the constitution of the Campus Tribunal must be approved by a two-thirds vote of the Student Senate.

RELEVANT CASE MATERIALS

First Amendment—Restraint of Expression

Hammond v. South Carolina State College
272 Fed. Supp. 947
Aug. 31, 1967

Hemphill, District Judge

Plaintiffs Hammond, Stroman and Bryant, Jr., seek protection of their individual and collective constitutional rights. On February 28, 1967, while enrolled as students in South Carolina State College in Orangeburg they "assembled themselves with numerous other students . . . upon the campus of said college . . . and expressed themselves . . . concerning certain practices then in existence at said college." On February 24, 1967, each received a communication from the Dean of Students which read:

You are directed to meet the Faculty Discipline Committee in my office, Room 207, Mechanical Building, at 2:15 p.m. today, February 24, 1967, to answer charges that you were in violation of College regulations, specifically #1, under 4, page 49 of the Student Handbook which reads . . . The student body or any part of the student body is not to celebrate, parade or demonstrate on the campus at any time without the approval of the Office of the President. The Board of Trustees meeting in March of 1960 went on record as disapproving of demonstrations which involve violation of laws or of College regulations, or which disrupt the normal College routine.

Thereafter, as directed, they severally met with the Faculty Discipline Committee. After the meetings each plaintiff was advised:

Reference is made to the Discipline Committee hearing held in my office this afternoon on a report brought through the Office of the Dean of Students that you violated Rule 1, under 4, page 49 of the College Handbook by participating in a demonstration on campus without approval.

The Committee feels that it gave you ample opportunity to refute the charge, but your refusal to do so left it no alternative but to take action.

The Committee has instructed me to inform you that its decision is that you be indefinitely suspended from the College effective February 24, 1967, until August 1, 1970. On or after that date (August 1, 1970) you may reapply for admission, but readmission shall depend upon unanimous approval of the Discipline Committee in full session assembled.

In accordance with the suspension you are to remain away from the campus until the end of the suspension period.

A requested rehearing with the Faculty Discipline Committee was held on March 2, 1967, and they were advised that the suspension was to remain in effect, but that each could apply for readmittance in August, 1967. Suit was commenced March 10, 1967. On March 15, 1967, plaintiffs filed Petition for a Temporary Restraining Order, and the same day this court ordered their readmittance pendente lite and ruled defendant to show cause why the suspensions should not be enjoined. . . .

(1) Defendant initially challenges the jurisdiction of this court. The issue is not seriously pressed. Plaintiffs complain that defendant has deprived them of their rights under the First Amendment to the Constitution of the United States, and have done so by virtue of the authority or color of office enjoyed by the administrators and faculty of defendant. Defendant is a state institution and its administrative personnel are vested with state authority. . . .

The facts which are not in dispute are essentially as follows.

On February 23, 1967, these three plaintiffs in the company of approximately three hundred others gathered together on the campus of the school to express their feelings regarding some of the school's practices.

This, they claim, they did in an orderly and peaceful fashion. The school, however, maintains that the plaintiffs were leaders of the demonstration and that it was noisy and disorderly.

The plaintiffs were unquestionably aware of the rule against unauthorized demonstrations. However, on February 21, 1967, the President of the institution had delivered a written report publicly assuring the students that no rule deprived them of the constitutional rights of free speech and of peaceable assembly.

According to their testimony to the Faculty Discipline Committee on that day, they received the notice only a matter of several hours prior to the meeting.

At the Discipline Committee hearing each of them objected to the notice given and refused to answer questions on the grounds that they desired the assistance of counsel. One felt that he might incriminate himself. They demanded to be confronted with their accusers and to be allowed to cross-examine them.

The Faculty Discipline Committee was not disposed to postpone the hearing to allow time for counsel nor was it disposed to allow confrontation and cross-examination of the witnesses. The plaintiffs, however, did establish that they were participants in an assembly and that in exercising the right to do so they would deny having violated Rule 1.

The same date all of the plaintiffs were notified as to their suspensions as set forth above.

The school's Board of Trustees had in March of 1960 passed the following resolution in the avowed interest of protecting the "students of this institution from violence and to preserve public peace and order."

Be It Resolved that hereafter any student at South Carolina State College who shall engage in any public demonstrations without prior approval of the College administration shall be summarily expelled.

The controversy here revolves around the school rules of deportment and discipline. Their obvious purpose is to protect the authority and administrative responsibility which is imposed on the officers of the institution. Unless the officials have authority to keep order, they have no power to guarantee education. If they cannot preserve order by rule and regulation, and insist on obedience to those rules, they will be helpless in the face of the mob, powerless to command or rebuke the fanatic, the irritant, the malingerer, the rabble rouser. To be sure, this is a tax supported institution, but this does not give license to chaos, or the hope to create chaos. The majority of the taxpayers who established, through representative government, the institution, and all the taxpayers who support this institution, have a vested interest in a peaceful campus, an academic climate of order and culture. The power of the president to oversee, to rule, is an integral part of the mechanism for providing and promoting education at State College. Be that as it may, colleges, like all other institutions, are subject to the Constitution. Academic progress and academic freedom demand their share of Constitutional protection. Here we find a clash between the Rules of the school and the First Amendment to the Constitution of the United States.

(2, 3) The First Amendment does not speak equivocally. It prohibits any law "abridging the freedom of speech, or of the press. It must be taken as a command of the broadest scope that explicit language, read in the context of a liberty-loving society, will allow." . . . These rights of the First Amendment, including the right to peaceably assemble, are not to be restricted except upon the showing of a clear and present danger, of riot, disorder or immediate threat to public safety, peace or order. . . . "Only the gravest abuses, endangering paramount interests, give occasion for permissible limitation." . . . Conduct which involves activities such as picketing and marching, however, is a departure from the exercise of the rights in pristine form and it does not receive the same degree of freedom. . . . It has been argued to me that Rule 1 of the Student Handbook as it is written is a previous restraint upon these rights and as such it is unlawful and must be struck down as being "incompatible with the guarantees of the first amendment." . . . I am persuaded that Rule 1 is on its face a prior restraint on the right to freedom to speech and the right to assemble. The rule does not purport to prohibit assemblies which have qualities that are unacceptable to responsible standards of conduct: it prohibits "parades, celebrations and demonstrations" without prior approval without any regard to limiting its proscription to assemblies involving misconduct or disruption of government activities or nonpeaceable gatherings. On this ground I do not feel that it is necessary to make a finding as to the nature of the demonstration. It was alleged by the defendant that the students were suspended not under Rule 1 but under Rule 4, presumably a rule covering misconduct. It may well be that the conduct of these students would have warranted disciplinary action under some disciplinary rule such as Rule 4[4] but in point of fact they were not suspended under Rule 4. They were charged under Rule 1, they were given hearings under Rule 1, and they were suspended under Rule 1.

In no way is it my intention to rule that school officials may not make disciplinary rules and enforce them. Most certainly they may. I am constrained to rule, however, that the rule under which these students were suspended was incompatible with the constitutional guarantees and is invalid.

The defendant has argued that it, no less than a private citizen, has the right to control the use of its property, and that . . . no one has the right to demonstrate at any time at any place he may choose. The campus, under his argument, being dedicated to scholarship and learning would be likened to a hospital or the jail entrance . . . and prohibiting demonstrations would, similarly, not infringe any constitutional rights. In principle the argument is unassailable; however, it does not apply to this case. The rule broadly brings the entire campus of a state college within its ambit . . . that assembling at the site of government for peaceful expression of grievances constituted exercise of First Amendment rights in their pristine form. I am not persuaded that the campus of a state college is not similarly available for the same purposes for its students.

Therefore . . . I find that the suspension of the students was unlawful and cannot be given effect. This, of course, does not mean that the school may not institute proper disciplinary proceedings against the students for lack of [proper] deportment and violations of other appropriate disciplinary regulations.

I therefore order that the defendants be permanently enjoined from enforcing the decisions of the Faculty Discipline Committee which dismissed these plaintiffs for breach of Rule 1 of Part 4 of the Student Handbook.

And it is so ordered.

---

4. For instance, rule 13 provides: students are expected to conduct themselves as ladies and gentlemen at all times. Boisterousness, profanity, insubordination, unkempt appearances and any other undesirable quality will not be tolerated and is not expected of students at the College.

First Amendment—Student Publications
PAPISH
v.
BOARD OF CURATORS OF UNIVERSITY OF MISSOURI
93 S. Ct. 1197, 1973.

Decided March 19, 1973.

Per Curiam.

Petitioner, a graduate student in the University of Missouri School of Journalism, was expelled for distributing on campus a newspaper "containing forms of indecent speech" in violation of the By-Laws of the Board of Curators. The newspaper, the Free Press Underground, had been sold on this state university campus for more than four years pursuant to an authorization obtained from the University Business Office. The particular newspaper issue in question was found to be unacceptable for two reasons. First, on the front cover the publishers had reproduced a political cartoon previously printed in another newspaper depicting policemen raping the Statue of Liberty and the Goddess of Justice. The caption under the cartoon read: ". . . With Liberty and Justice for All." Secondly, the issue contained an article entitled "M - - - - - - f - - - - - - Acquitted," which discussed the trial and acquittal on an assault charge of a New York City youth who was a member of an organization known as "Up Against the Wall, M - - - - - - f - - - - - -."

(1) Following a hearing, the Student Conduct Committee found that petitioner had violated Paragraph B of Art. A of the General Standards of Student Conduct which requires students "to observe generally accepted standards of conduct" and specifically prohibits "indecent conduct or speech." Her dismissal, after affirmance first by the Chancellor of the University and then by its Board of Curators, was made effective in the middle of the spring semester. Although she was then permitted to remain on campus until the end of the semester, she was not given credit for the one course in which she made a passing grade.

After exhausting her administrative review alternatives within the University, petitioner brought an action for declaratory and injunctive relief pursuant to 42 U. S. C. §1983 in the United States District Court for the Western District of Missouri. She claimed that her dismissal was improperly premised on activities protected by the First Amendment. The District Court denied relief, 331 F.

Supp. 1321, and the Court of Appeals affirmed, one judge dissenting, 464 F. 2d 136. Rehearing en banc was denied by an equally divided vote of all the judges in the Eighth Circuit.

The District Court's opinion rests, in part, on the conclusion that the banned issue of the newspaper was obscene. The Court of Appeals found it unnecessary to decide that question. Instead, assuming that the newspaper was not obscene and that its distribution in the community at large would be protected by the First Amendment, the court held that on a university campus "freedom of expression" could properly be "subordinated to other interests such as, for example, the conventions of decency in the use and display of language and pictures." The court concluded that "[t]he Constitution does not compel the University [to allow] such publications as the one in litigation to be publicly sold or distributed on its open campus."

(2-4) This case was decided several days before we handed down Healy v. James, 408 U. S. 169, 1972, in which, while recognizing a state university's undoubted prerogative to enforce reasonable rules governing student conduct, we reaffirmed that "state colleges and universities are not enclaves immune from the sweep of the First Amendment." . . . We think Healy makes it clear that the mere dissemination of ideas—no matter how offensive to good taste—on a state university campus may not be shut off in the name alone of "conventions of decency." Other recent precedents of this Court make it equally clear that neither the political cartoon nor the headline story involved in this case can be labelled as constitutionally obscene or otherwise unprotected. . . . There is language in the opinion below which suggests that the University's action here could be viewed as an exercise of its legitimate authority to enforce reasonable regulations as to the time, place and manner of speech and its dissemination. While we have repeatedly approved such regulatory authority . . . the facts set forth in the opinions below show clearly that petitioner was dismissed because of the disapproved content of the newspaper rather than the time, place or manner of its distribution.

(5, 6) Since the first Amendment leaves no room for the operation of a dual standard in the academic community with respect to the content of speech, and because the state University's action here cannot be justified as a nondiscriminatory application of reasonable rules governing conduct, the judgments of the courts below must be reversed. Accordingly the petition for a writ of certiorati is granted, the case is remanded to the District Court, and that court is instructed to order the University to restore to petitioner any course credits she earned for the semester in question and, unless she is barred from reinstatement for valid academic reasons, to reinstate her as a student in the graduate program.

Reversed and remanded.

First Amendment—Freedom of Association

Catherine J. Healy, et al., Petitioners

v.

F. Don James, et al.
408 U. S. 169 1972.
Argued March 28, 1972.
Decided June 26, 1972.

Mr. Justice Powell, A. J., S. Ct., delivered the opinion of the Court.

This case, arising out of a denial by a state college of official recognition to a group of students who desired to form a local chapter of Students for a Democratic Society (SDS), presents this Court with questions requiring the application of well-established First Amendment principles.

Petitioners are students attending Central Connecticut State College (CCSC), a state-supported institution of higher learning. In September, 1969, they undertook to organize what they then referred to as a "local chapter" of Students for a Democratic Society (SDS). Pursuant to procedures established by the College, petitioners filed a request for official recognition as a campus organization with the Student Affairs Committee, a committee composed of four students, three faculty members and the Dean of Student Affairs. The request specified three purposes for the proposed organization's existence. It would provide "a forum of discussion and self-education for students developing an analysis of American society"; it would serve as "an agency for integrating thought with action so as to bring about constructive changes"; and it would endeavor to provide "a coordinating body for relating the problems of leftist students" with other interested groups on campus and in the community. The Committee, while satisfied that the statement of purposes was clear and unobjectionable on its face, exhibited concern over the relationship between the proposed local group and the

National SDS organization. In response to inquiries, representatives of the proposed organization stated that they would not affiliate with any national organization and that their group would remain "completely independent."

By a vote of six to two the Committee ultimately approved the application and recommended to the President of the College, Dr. James, that the organization be accorded official recognition. . . . Several days later, the President rejected the Committee's recommendation, and issued a statement indicating that petitioners' organization was not to be accorded the benefits of official campus recognition.

Denial of official recognition posed serious problems for the organization's existence and growth. Its members were deprived of the opportunity to place announcements regarding meetings, rallies or other activities in the student newspaper; they were precluded from using various campus bulletin boards; and, most importantly, nonrecognition barred them from using campus facilities for holding meetings.

(1) At the outset we note that state colleges and universities are not enclaves immune from the sweep of the First Amendment. "It can hardly be argued that either students or teachers shed their constitutional rights to freedom of speech or expression at the schoolhouse gate." . . . The precedents of this Court leave no room for the view that, because of the acknowledged need for order, First Amendment protections should apply with less force on college campuses than in the community at large. Quite to the contrary, "[t]he vigilant protection of constitutional freedoms is nowhere more vital than in the community of American schools." Shelton v. Tucker, 364 U. S. 479, 487, 81 S. Ct. 247, 251, 5 L. Ed. 2d 231 (1960). The college classroom with its surrounding environs is peculiarly the "market place of ideas" and we break no new constitutional ground in reaffirming this Nation's dedication to safeguarding academic freedom.

(4) Petitioners' associational interests also were circumscribed by the denial of the use of campus bulletin boards and the school newspaper. If any organization is to remain a viable entity in a campus community in which new students enter on a regular basis, it must possess the means of communicating with these students. Moreover, the organization's ability to participate in the intellectual give and take of campus debate and to pursue its stated purposes is

limited by denial of access to the customary media for communicating with the administration, faculty members and other students. Such impediments cannot be viewed as insubstantial.

(17-20) . . . The critical line for First Amendment purposes must be drawn between advocacy, which is entitled to full protection, and action, which is not. Petitioners may, if they so choose, preach the propriety of amending or even doing away with any or all campus regulations. They may not, however, undertake to flout these rules. Mr. Justice Blackmun, at the time he was a circuit judge on the Eighth Circuit, stated:

"We . . . hold that a college has the inherent power to promulgate rules and regulations; that it has the inherent power properly to discipline; that it has power appropriately to protect itself and its property; that it may expect that its students adhere to generally accepted standards of conduct." Esteban v. Central Missouri State College, 415 F. 2d 1077, 1089 (CA8 1969), cert. denied, 398 U. S. 965, 90 S. Ct. 2169, 26 L. Ed. 2d 548 (1970).

Just as in the community at large, reasonable regulations with respect to the time, the place and the manner in which student groups conduct their speech-related activities must be respected. A college administration may impose a requirement, such as may have been imposed in this case, that a group seeking official recognition affirm in advance its willingness to adhere to reasonable campus law. Such a requirement does not impose an impermissible condition of the students' associational rights. Their freedom to speak out, to assemble or to petition for changes in school rules is in no sense infringed. It merely constitutes an agreement to conform with reasonable standards respecting conduct. This is a minimal requirement, in the interest of the entire academic community, of any group seeking the privileges of official recognition.

(21) Petitioners have not challenged in this litigation the procedural or substantive aspects of the College's requirements governing applications for official recognition. Although the record is unclear on this point, CCSC may have, among its requirements for recognition, a rule that prospective groups affirm that they intend to comply with reasonable campus regulations. Upon remand it should first be determined whether the College recognition procedures contemplate any such requirement. If so, it should then be ascertain whether petitioners intend to comply. Since we do not have the terms of a specific prior affirmation rule before us, we

are not called on to decide whether any particular formulation would or would not prove constitutionally acceptable. Assuming the existence of a valid rule, however, we do conclude that the benefits of participation in the internal life of the college community may be denied to any group that reserves the right to violate any valid campus rules with which they disagree.

We think the above discussion established the appropriate framework for consideration of petitioners' request for campus recognition. Because respondents failed to accord due recognition to First Amendment principles, the judgment below approving respondents' denial of recognition must be reversed. Since we cannot conclude from this record that petitioners were willing to abide by reasonable campus rules and regulations, we order the case remanded for reconsideration. We note, in so holding, that the wide latitude accorded by the Constitution to the freedoms of expression and association is not without its costs in terms of the risk to the maintenance of civility and an ordered society. Indeed, this latitude often has resulted, on the campus and elsewhere, in the infringement of the rights of others. Though we deplore the tendency of some to abuse the very constitutional privileges they invoke, and although the infringement of rights of others certainly should not be tolerated, we reaffirm this Court's dedication to the principles of the Bill of Rights upon which our vigorous and free society is founded.

CHAPTER VI

Conclusions

The society that relies on its judiciary for the resolution of its fundamental social and economic problems has doomed itself to failure. The judiciary is capable of protecting individuals against the tyranny of the majority, at least for a short while. It is capable of aiding in the effectuation of fundamental social and economic alterations in that society's fabric, once society has started on that task. It is even capable of suggesting to that society those changes which it may choose to adopt. But if its strength is its political irresponsibility, so too is that its weakness. We can ignore this lesson of history only at the price of watching an impotent judiciary issue unenforceable edicts while the nation is fragmented by conflicts not subjugable by the judicial fiat. We cannot afford to try to avoid our troubles by asking the judiciary to cure them (Page 67).[5]

D EVELOPING UNEQUIVOCAL LEGAL responses to educational controversies is fraught with difficulty. Questions of educational jurisdiction and judgement are not easily amenable to either judicial procedures or decrees. Simply put, the law is not a science, and may not be even an art.[6] In fact, controversies brought to the judiciary do not always result in decisions which meet the needs of the parties involved, or can even be enforced.[7]

Although the Supreme Court has argued that a defendant must be supplied with a lawyer if he cannot hire his own, nonetheless, it is true that not all lawyers are of equal competence and dedication. It is also true that the problem of equal educational opportunity addressed and supposedly answered in *Brown v. The Board of Education* (351 U. S. at 23 1954) still remains unresolved, that is, today more blacks attend school with other blacks than in 1954. In *Brown,* the court asked that school desegregation be

---

5. Charles V. Daly, Editor, *The Quality of Inequality: Urban and Suburban Public Schools* (University of Chicago, 1968) , p. 67.

6. Ibid., p. 47.

7. Ibid., p. 58.

implemented with all deliberate speed. The court's decree remains ineffectual and unenforceable because communities in almost every area of the country disagree with the Court's policy pronouncement. If, then, a decision of the court faces community opposition, it is likely that the execution of that decision will be difficult and the impact of that decision will be negligible.[8]

Judicial policy-making, moreover, has a profound political impact. In *Brown,* the court declared the separate but equal doctrine unconstitutional when applied to public education. As a result of the Court's decision, some communities moved to realign school districts so as to achieve racial integration. Other communities attempted to abolish public school systems in order to circumvent the Court's decree.[9]

Questions regarding a student's educational growth, i.e. his intellectual and personal progress, are necessarily questions which require evaluation and qualitative judgement. The former President of Cornell University, James A. Perkins, has noted that civil laws cannot easily resolve questions requiring qualitative decisions.[10] Courts and their complex procedures militate against the kind of humanistic process needed in educational decision-making. Resort to the court for solutions to questions relating to intellectual inquiry, moreover, can lead only to costly delay in the resolving of individual or institutional problems. Ultimately, there is grave danger to student-teacher relationships when and if those relationships must conform to civil jurisdiction, rather than academic norms. Such norms include personal and intellectual relationships which would be chilled by the formalities of the law.

The counseling relationship, indeed, cannot be subject to civil jurisdiction if it is to be effective. If the function of a college is to help individuals grow and develop a clear sense of meaning in their own lives, then it is critically important to limit the kinds of formal procedures and rules made necessary by resort to the court.

8. Charles V. Daly, Editor, *The Quality of Inequality: Urban and Suburban Public Schools* (University of Chicago, 1968) , p. 59.

9. Victor G. Rosenblum, *Law as a Political Instrument* (New York: Random House, 1961) , p. 65.

10. See James A. Perkins, "The University and Due Process," *Chronicle of the American Council on Education* (Washington, D. C., 1967, pp. 7-9) .

It is unlikely that educational institutions can maintain the initiative to create new educational forms if they are at the same time compelled to impose a super structure of civil jurisdiction upon personal and intellectual relationships. If student personnel administrators believe that education becomes more meaningful as face-to-face relationships among students, faculty members and administrators are increased, then resort to the anonymity of the law may be most often inappropriate.

The lowering of the voting age to eighteen suggests new political, economic and legal realities for the college student. A student personnel administrator should be ready to work with students so that they may develop those interpersonal and vocational skills necessary to meet the demands of a changing society. Such administrators must attempt wherever possible to utilize institutional resources in order to resolve the problems of individuals who live and work within the academic context. It is foolish to argue that colleges and universities are separate from communities in which they live, but at the same time institutional integrity and purpose should not be compromised by inviting civil jurisdiction in those matters of intellectual and personal inquiry which are best left to educators themselves.

It can be argued that politics can never be separate from educational institutions, particularly because such institutions, both public and private, continue to seek local, state and federal government relief in the form of tax abatement, municipal and state services and, of course, public funding. Given the political implications of judicial action and the obvious political and financial ties to governments that an educational institution must maintain, it is important to recognize the fundamental dilemma faced by the student personnel administrator. As an educator, he has a professional obligation to promote among students a knowledge of self and others. He must encourage self-direction and an informed sense of legal, social and economic realities. The immediate political and legal consequences of a student's activity, however, may limit almost instantly the educative role of the dean. If the dean is to be more than a fountain of legal wisdom to be used by students in trouble, if he is to be more than a supportive albeit older friend, if he is to be more than a tarnished professional looking for a role to play, he must begin to define the values and goals to be embodied by his institution in a way which will be relevant and meaningful to all members of the university community; he must try to mediate and reconcile the inevitable conflicts among interests, particularly in financially pressing times; he must aid in maximizing the well-being of individuals as well as the development of his institution; and he must further attempt to sensitize and alert the entire community to the present and future kinds of social, economic and legal conditions likely to shape his institution's direction. The behavioral sciences background of many student personnel officers will be particularly helpful in initiating the kinds of institutional studies that will become necessary.

The concept of the student personnel administrator as unifier, mediator and teacher within the college community diverges dramatically from more orthodox and traditional views of the administrator as disciplinarian, housekeeper and lord of the realm all rolled into one. It calls for personal qualities of sensitivity, intelligence and awareness which administrators up to this time have rarely been called upon to exercise, and which some will have difficulty in ever finding.

The Courts will continue to examine whether educational institutions have the authority to take particular kinds of action, legislatures will continue to approve legislation which fund educational institutions, legal conditions of both the common law and statutory variety will continue to be made. It is critically important, however, that the Student Personnel Administrator view the law in the context of his own institution and educational role, that of unifier, mediator and teacher. Questions of the qualitative kind, questions of discretion and judgment can then be made to the advantage of both individual and institution.

CHAPTER VII

Further Aspects of Concern to Student Personnel Administrators

T HE FOLLOWING TOPICS, although not of sufficient scope to warrant inclusion in preceding chapters, nevertheless, are significant in and of themselves and should be considered problem areas by the Student Personnel Administrator.

STUDENTS, WORK-RELATED INJURIES, AND THE LAW

A brief synopsis of a model Workmen's Compensation Act as it might relate to student employees follows:

Legal Memorandum

A state's Workmen's Compensation Act is legislation of enlightened social significance and applies broadly to all employees who are under its jurisdiction. This includes injuries suffered in or outside the state if the contract of employment was made within the state.

When personal injury is caused to an employee by accident arising out of and in the course of his employment, he shall receive compensation, therefor, from his employer, provided the injury was not intentionally self-inflicted, a result of horseplay he initiated or a concomitant of being inebriated.

The broadest possible interpretation is given this act to aid a workman to recover. Although the Workmen's Compensation Act is in derogation of the common law, it is to be liberally construed, Sharp v. Borough of Vineland, 118 NJL 567 (1936).

Consequently, the burden of proof is always on the employer when he contests jurisdiction or the right of the workman to recover. There is no paucity of unusual or even bizarre cases where recovery was granted even though by all logical standards the employee was not so entitled. This is probably a result of the positional or "but for" test which has been adopted in most states. This test connotes a standard of reasonable probability, the question being whether it is more probably true than not that the injury would have occurred during the time and place of employment rather than elsewhere.

The right to compensation acts as a surrender by the parties, thereto, of their rights to any other method. If injury or death is compensable under this act, the employer shall not be liable to anyone at common law or otherwise. Recovery will be limited to this statute.

The employee shall further not be barred in his attempt for recovery by contributory negligence, assumption of risk or the fellow servant rule.

If a contract of hiring, expressly in writing, signed by both parties, indicates that the Workmen's Compensation Act shall not apply, then common law remedies and defenses shall be reserved.

With regard to the employment of minors, the Workmen's Compensation Act shall apply. If the injured employee at the time of the accident is a minor under fourteen years of age, employed in violation of the labor law, or a minor between fourteen to eighteen years of age, employed or permitted to work without an employment certificate, or at an occupation prohibited by the minor's age by law, a compensation or death benefit shall be payable to the employee or his dependents which shall be double the amount ordinarily so payable under the schedules of the Act. This extra compensation will be imposed only against the employer and not the insurance carrier, indemnifying agreements notwithstanding.

It must be noted that nothing in this statute shall deprive an infant under the age of eighteen years to alternately choose to recover damages in common law for the negligence of his or her master. In given circumstances a civil recovery in negligence could greatly exceed the amount which would be awarded in the schedules of the Workmen's Compensation Act.

When a compensible injury occurs, the employer must furnish to the injured workman such medical, surgical and other treatment and hospital service as shall be authorized and necessary to cure and restore the functions of the injured member or again where such restoration is possible.

There is a seven-day waiting period for compensation other than medical and during which time the employee is unable to continue work. Should the total period of disability extend beyond seven days, then compensation shall be payable covering the entire period including the waiting period.

There are four basic divisions in the wage and compensation schedule. One is concerned with temporary disability benefits, another with permanent total disability, the third with permanent partial disability and the last with death benefits.

For the time period the employee is unable to work by virtue of his injury, he shall be entitled to temporary disability benefits computed as 66⅔ percent of the weekly wages received at the time of the injury. The minimum so paid shall be $15.00 per week and the maximum of 66⅔ percent of the average weekly wages earned by all employees covered by Unemployment Compensation. The period such compensation shall be paid will not extend beyond 300 weeks.

If the employee has been disabled totally in character and permanently in quality he shall be entitled to 66⅔ percent of his weekly wages received at the time of the injury or a minimum of $15.00 per week for a period of 450 weeks. Suitable extensions beyond this period are possible.

For disability partial in character and permanent in quality, compensation shall be based upon a schedule starting at a minimum of $10.00 per week to a maximum of $40.00 per week. The compensation is computed according to the wages paid at the time of the injury from the law of $10.00 compensation for a $15.00 weekly wage to a maximum of $40.00 compensation per week for a weekly wage of $67.51 and over.

For orthopedic and psychiatric injuries, the compensation is computed by taking a percentage of 550 weeks times the weekly wage entitled to. For example if a workman earning $100.00 per week sustained neurological disability partial in character and permanent in quality to the extent of 5 percent, he would receive 27½ weeks at $40.00 per week or $1100.00. The percentage is arrived at by the deliberations of the respective attorneys, forensic physicians and the workman's compensation judge or referee.

For a member of the body lost, compensation is based upon a specific schedule. For example loss of a thumb entitles the workman to permanent partial disability in the amount of seventy-five weeks times $40.00 or $3000.00 (based on the maximum wage of $67.51 per week, at the time of the injury).

If death results during the period of payments other than by accident or occupational disease the remaining payments are made to the workman's dependents. If no dependents are so entitled, a maximum of $750.00 will be paid in a lump sum to the proper person for death benefits.

Death benefits for workmen who die because of accident or occupational disease are paid to dependents according to a schedule which awards a maximum of 450 weeks at 66⅔ percent of the average weekly wages received at the time of injury subject to the aforestated maximum. Compensation for dependents under eighteen shall continue after such period according to the number of such dependents until the age of eighteen years is reached.

In conclusion, since the benefits that could be awarded a student-employee would vary greatly according to circumstance, it would be virtually impossible to determine before the injury, and judicial determination whether the benefits to be awarded would be morally sufficient.

Consequently, it is recommended that a fund be implemented which could supplement Workman Compensation payments when the amount awarded to a student-worker would be determined insufficient because of his minimal wage. Whether such fund should be created, how it would be administered, etc., is the proper subject for each Dean of Students and his student-staff-faculty advisory groups.

Questions regarding insurance coverage for student employees:

1. If a student works in a nonrecurring type of job for the University for a period of a couple of days or a couple of hours per year and is paid by Payroll, is he covered automatically under Workmen's Compensation Insurance?
2. If a student is paid out of petty cash or on a stipend basis, is he still automatically covered by Workmen's Compensation Insurance?
3. Students are employed by the student activities department and are paid directly by student activities. (Student activities have their own checking account.) Such students are not reflected on the university payroll records. Would they be covered by Workmen's Compensation Insurance?
4. Some students have fellowships, and are both students and employees of the university. They are paid by accounts payable, and not by the payroll department. Are they covered under Workmen's Compensation?
5. Are students who travel on university business by various means— car, bus, train, plane—covered by Workmen's Compensation and personal tort liability insurance?

6. Are student employees covered by Workmen's Compensation and individual tort liability insurance when operating a university vehicle? Are student employees covered by Workmen's Compensation and individual tort liability insurance when operating privately owned vehicles?

STUDENT EMPLOYEES AND COLLECTIVE BARGAINING

Student employees, whether clerical or paraprofessionals, whose employment is incidental to their educational objectives, generally will be excluded from collective bargaining units. Resident assistants, gameroom attendants and other staff assistants who obtain employment through student service directors rather than a universiy's personnel office are said to lack a community of interest with other employees.

UNITED STATES OF AMERICA
BEFORE THE NATIONAL LABOR RELATIONS BOARD

BARNARD COLLEGE
                Employer
        and   Case 2—RC—16011
DISTRICT 65, DISTRIBUTIVE
WORKERS OF AMERICA
                Petitioner

DECISION ON REVIEW

On March 7, 1973, the Regional Director for Region 2 issued a Decision and Direction of Election in the above-entitled proceeding wherein he included, among others, ten student employees in a unit of office clerical and other nonprofessional administrative staff employees which he found appropriate. Thereafter, in accordance with Section 102.67 of the National Labor Relations Board's Rules and Regulations, the Employer filed a timely request for review in which it contended, inter alia, that the Regional Director, by including the disputed student employees, departed from reported precedent.[11]

---

11. The following institutions submitted briefs in support of the request for review: New York University; American Council on Education; Cornell University; Adelphi University; Columbia University; Mount Holyoke College; Wellesley College; Fordham University; Boston University; Duke University; University of Wisconsin; Pennsylvania State University; and Amherst College.

By telegraphic order dated April 13, 1973, the National Labor Relations Board granted the request for review as to the students but directed that the scheduled election proceed with the students being permitted to vote under challenge, and that, at the conclusion of the balloting, all ballots were to be impounded pending decision on review.

Pursuant to the provisions of Section 3(b) of the National Labor Relations Act, as amended, the National Labor Relations Board has delegated its authority in this proceeding to a three-member panel.

The Board has considered the entire record in this case, including the briefs on review,[12] and makes the following findings:

The Employer is a private nonprofit educational institution located in New York City with an enrollment of approximately 2,000 students. It contends that the student employees included in the unit by the Regional Director lack a community of interest with the other unit employees. The unit is office clerical and other nonprofessional administrative staff employees. We agree.

At issue herein are six graduate assistants employed in the residence halls, two undergraduate students who work as typists in the college activities office, and two graduate students employed as desk attendants at the bowling alley and the entrance to the college activities building. All the foregoing positions are reserved specifically for students and, in the instance of the residence hall graduate assistants, enrollment in a graduate program and prior experience in residence halls are specific prerequisites for the position.

Unlike other employees in the unit who obtain employment through the Employer's personnel office, the graduate assistants are hired directly by the resident directors, and the other students obtain their positions through the student placement office. Normally, the student employees are employed on a semester or academic year basis and do not work during school vacation periods, the summer period, or after they leave school. The graduate assistants are paid a $1,000 or $1,500 stipend and are provided rooms at the residence hall where they are required to live. The students at the college activities building and office are paid from $2 to $2.50 per hour which appears to be substantially below the hourly rate

---

12. Wheaton College of Norton, Massachusetts, with permission of the Board, filed a brief as *amicus curiae* which has also been considered.

of other employees including in the unit. None of the disputed student employees receive the usual fringe benefits normally received by the full-time and regular part-time employees. The graduate assistants work on an "on call" basis between 5:00 p.m. and 8:00 a.m., performing emergency services in the absence of the resident directors, such as taking students to the hospital, calling police in case of intruders, or counseling students concerning academic or family problems. The students in the college activities building are employed during the evening hours principally to oversee the use of equipment and facilities.[13] The students in the college activities office work during the normal daytime hours as their class schedules permit. The only apparent distinction between the two student employees in the college activities office included by the Regional Director and the three other students employed there who were excluded, is the fact that the former happened to work between fifteen and twenty hours per week while the latter work fewer than fifteen hours per week.[14]

Although it is true, as the Regional Director found, that the student employees herein are subject to the same supervision as the nonstudent employees and have some contacts in their work with the latter, it is clear from the foregoing facts that the student employees are treated differently in a number of significant ways, especially with respect to their initial employment, rates of pay, tenure and other employment conditions. Indeed, other than the fact that some of the disputed student employees happen to work a few more hours per week than those student employees excluded by stipulation, the record does not support the conclusion

13. Although the two students currently employed in these positions are not Barnard students, the record shows the incumbents are treated in the same manner as other students employees with respect to their wages, hours and conditions of employment.

However, Member Fanning would include in the unit regular part-time employees who are not students at Barnard or Columbia. This is in accord with Board practice to include in units, generally, students who work as regular part-time employees during the school year. See Giordano Lumber Co., Inc., 133 NLRB 205, 207.

14. The parties stipulated that all employees employed fifteen or fewer hours per week are casual employees. Approximately 150 other student employees were excluded as a result of this stipulation. Barnard students are generally subject to an academic policy which does not permit them to work more than fifteen hours per week. The Employer asserts the disputed employees in the college activities office were permitted to work more than fifteen hours due to an administrative oversight by that office in failing to adhere to the foregoing policy.

that the interests of both groups are significantly distinguishable. Moreover, as few, if any, student employees ever remain or are permitted to remain permanently in their present employment, it is clear that their employment here is only incidental to their educational objectives. Therefore, in accordance with our existing precedent, we shall exclude the ten disputed employees herein[15] and the challenge to their respective ballots is hereby sustained.

Accordingly, the unit found appropriate by the Regional Director is hereby modified to conform with this decision and the case is hereby remanded to the Regional Director for the purpose of counting the impounded ballots, issuing an appropriate tally of ballots, and for other appropriate action.

Dated, Washington, D. C. Jul. 17, 1973.

STUDENTS, OBSCENITY AND THE LAW

Criteria for determining criminal obscenity has suffered from changing judicial interpretation and social values. In 1957, the United States Supreme Court in Roth v. United States decided that obscenity was not protected by the First Amendment. The Court found that obscenity constituted material which lacked redeeming social importance. The Roth case was followed in 1966 by Memoirs v. Massachusetts where the Court required that, to prove obscenity, it must be affirmatively established that the material in question was without redeeming social value. Since Roth, there has never been a clear majority of the Court able to agree on what constitutes obscene or pornographic material. Nevertheless, tests of obscenity since 1966 have been as follows:

(1) the dominant theme of the material taken as a whole appeals to a prurient interest in sex;

(2) the material is patently offensive because it affronts contemporary community standards relating to the description or representation of sexual matters; and

(3) the material is utterly without redeeming social value.

However, in 1973, in Miller v. California and related cases, the Supreme Court handed down a new set of guidelines. Specifically,

---

15. Cornell University, 202 NLRB No. 41; Georgetown University, 200 NLRB No. 14. In view of our conclusion that the student employees herein do not have a sufficient community of interest with the nonstudent employees, we see no reason at this time to reach the contention made by Wheaton College in its *amicus curiae* brief that student employees employed by the institutions they attend are not employees within the meaning of Sec. 2 (3) of the Act.

the Court, speaking through Chief Justice Warren Burger, set new definitions for establishing obscenity:

(1) a state may punish the printing or sale of works which appeal to prurient interest in sex, which portray sexual conduct in a patently offensive way and which, taken as a whole, do not have serious literary, artistic, political or scientific value;

(2) that the view of average persons, applying contemporary community standards, be controlling in determining obscenity; and

(3) states must explicitly in their laws define violative sexual conduct which will be subject to prosecution.

The new standards articulated by the Court will now enable states to ban books, magazines, plays and motion pictures that are offensive to local standards even though such material may be acceptable elsewhere.

Educational institutions under the Burger obscenity guidelines do not appear to have immunity from local community standards that may prevail where such an institution is located. Educators, then, should adjust academic and personal programming to contemporary community standards.

Case Study

FACTS ABOUT HARRIET TOGETHER

Harriet Together, a freshman resident student, together with her floor counselor, decide to sponsor a sex education seminar for their residence complex. Harriet is able to secure, through her boyfriend's father, a stag film which she believes will add an educative and realistic element to their program. The Campus Provost, a former clergyman, learns that a stag film will be shown in the residence halls that night. He stops his work immediately and calls the Dean of Students.

Problem Analysis

The Dean of Students having learned of Harriet Together's intention to exhibit a stag film as part of a sex education seminar should consider relevant criminal law and campus regulations in making his decision. In this case there is no specific university regulation governing the exhibition of movies. The Dean, who cannot always be an expert in and be acquainted with appropriate law, should consult with his campus legal advisor in order to thereby examine municipal, state and federal laws regarding obscenity. The Dean should not depend upon his own knowledge and reading of newspaper or magazine articles which discuss court decisions and statutes.

Having discussed the matter of exhibition with counsel, the Dean learns that a state statute has defined obscene any book, writing or film which is:

(1) dominantly prurient.
(2) patently offends community standards.
(3) utterly without redeeming social value.

He also learns from counsel that a recent Supreme Court ruling held that the views of a local community on prurience were applicable in obscenity controversies. Redeeming social value, moreover, was no longer a defense to a prosecution for obscenity.

Counsel had advised, furthermore, that a state statute prohibits the utterance or exposure to view or hearing any obscene or indecent book, picture or mechanical recording upon penalty of being held guilty of a misdemeanor.

The Dean then calls in Harriet Together and explains on what basis he has made his decision.

Model State Statutes

2A:115-1.1 "Obscene" defined

(a) The word "obscene," wherever it appears in the chapter, to which this act is a supplement, shall mean that which to the average person, applying contemporary community standards, when considered as a whole, has as its dominant theme or purpose an appeal to prurient interest.

(b) Any book, publication, picture, writing, record or other mechanical or electronic audio or visual reproduction or other material shall be obscene within the meaning of subsection (a) hereof if it is established that:

(1) The dominant theme of the material taken as a whole appeals to the prurient interest;

(2) The material is patently offensive because it affronts contemporary community standards relating to the description or representation of sexual matters; and

(3) The material is utterly without redeeming social value. L. 1962, c. 165, 1. Amended by L. 1966, c. 199, 1, eff. July 21, 1966.

2A:115-2. Uttering or exposing obscene literature or pictures

Any person who, without just cause, utters or exposes to the view or hearing of another, or possesses with intent to utter or expose to the view or hearing of another, any obscene or indecent book, publication, pamphlet, picture or any mechanical or electronic recording on a record, tape, wire or other device, or other representation however made or any person who shall sell, import, print, publish, loan, give away, design, prepare, distribute or offer for sale any obscene or indecent book, publication, pamphlet, picture or other representation, however made, or who in any way advertises the same, or in any manner, whether by recommendation against its use or otherwise, gives any information how or where any of the same may be had, seen, heard, bought or sold, is guilty of a misdemeanor. Amended by L. 1957, c. 175, p. 617, 1; L. 1959, c. 97, p. 237, 1, eff. June 12, 1959.

RELEVANT CASE MATERIALS

First Amendment—Freedom of Expression (Obscenity)

MILLER v. CALIFORNIA

72 Sup. Ct. 6038
June 21, 1973
Burger, W., C. J., S. C.

This is one of a group of "obscenity-pornography" cases being reviewed by the Court in a re-examination of standards enunciated in earlier cases involving what Mr. Justice Harlan called "the intractable obscenity problem."

This case involves the application of a state's criminal obscenity statute to a situation in which sexually explicit materials have been thrust by aggressive sales action upon unwilling recipients who had in no way indicated any desire to receive such materials.

This Court has recognized that the states have a legitimate interest in prohibiting dissemination or exhibition of obscene material when the mode of dissemination carries with it a significant danger of offending the sensibilities of unwilling recipients or of exposure to juveniles.

It is in this context that we are called on to define the standards which must be used to identify obscene material that a state may regulate without infringing the First Amendment as applicable to the states through the Fourteenth Amendment.

Since the Court now undertakes to formulate standards more concrete than those in the past, it is useful for us to focus on two of the landmark cases in the somewhat tortured history of the Court's obscenity decisions.

In Roth v. United States (1957) the Court sustained a conviction under a federal statute punishing the mailing of "obscene, lewd, lascivious or filthy" materials. The key to that holding was the Court's rejection of the claim that obscene materials were protected by the First Amendment. Five Justices joined in the opinion stating:

> "All ideas having even the slightest redeeming social importance—unorthodox ideas, controversial ideas, even ideas hateful to the prevailing climate of opinion—have full protection of the [First Amendment] guarantees, unless excludable because they encroach upon the limited area of more important interest. But implicit in the history of the First Amendment is the rejection of obscenity as utterly without redeeming social importance.
>
> "There are certain well-defined and narrowly limited classes of speech, the prevention and punishment of which have never been thought to raise any constitutional problem. These include the lewd and obscene.
>
> "It has been well observed that such utterances are no essential part of any exposition of ideas, and are of such slight social value as a step to truth that any benefit that may be derived from them is clearly outweighed by the social interest in order and morality.
>
> "We hold that obscenity is not within the area of constitutionally protected speech or press."

Nine years later in Memoirs v. Massachusetts (1966), the Court veered sharply away from the Roth concept and, with only three Justices in the plurality opinion, articulated a new test of obscenity. The plurality held that under the Roth definition:

"As elaborated in subsequent cases, three elements must coalesce: it must be established that (a) the dominant theme of the material taken as a whole appeals to a prurient interest in sex; (b) the material is patently offensive because it affronts contemporary community standards relating to the description or representation of sexual matters; and (c) the material is utterly without redeeming social value."

While Roth presumed "obscenity" to be "utterly without redeeming social value," Memoirs required that to prove obscenity it must be affirmatively established that the material is "utterly without redeeming social value."

Apart from the initial formulation in the Roth case, no majority of the Court has at any time been able to agree on a standard to determine what constitutes obscene, pornographic material subject to regulation under the states' police power.

We have seen "a variety of views among the members of the Court unmatched in any other course of constitutional adjudication." This is not remarkable, for in the area of freedom of speech and press the courts must always remain sensitive to any infringement on genuinely serious literary, artistic, political or scientific expression. This is an area in which there are few eternal verities.

This much has been categorically settled by the Court: that obscene material is unprotected by the First Amendment.

We acknowledge, however, the inherent dangers of undertaking to regulate any form of expression. State statutes designed to regulate obscene materials must be carefully limited. As a result, we now confine the permissible scope of such regulations to works which depict or describe sexual conduct.

That conduct must be specifically defined by the applicable state law, as written or authoritatively construed. A state offense must also be limited to works which, taken as a whole, appeal to the pruient interest in sex, which portray sexual conduct in a patently offensive way, and which, taken as a whole, do not have serious literary, artistic, political or scientific value.

The basic guidelines for the tryer of fact must be: (a) whether "the average person, applying contemporary community standards," would find that the work, taken as a whole, appeals to the prurient interest; (b) whether the work depicts or describes, in a patently offensive way, sexual conduct specifically defined by the applicable state law, and (c) whether the work, taken as a whole, lacks serious literary, artistic, political or scientific value.

We do not adopt as a constitutional standard the "utterly without redeeming social value" test. That concept has never commanded the adherence of more than three justices at one time. If a state law that regulates obscene material is thus limited, as written or construed, the First Amendment values applicable to the states through the Fourteenth Amendment are adequately protected by the ultimate power of appellate courts to conduct an independent review of constitutional claims when necessary.

We emphasize that it is not our function to propose regulatory schemes for the states. It is possible, however, to give a few plain examples of what a state statute could define for regulation under the second part (b) of the standard announced in this opinion:

(A) Patently offensive representations or descriptions of ultimate sexual acts, normal or perverted, actual or simulated.

(B) Patently offensive representations or descriptions of masturbation, excretory functions and lewd exhibition of the genitals.

Sex and nudity may not be exploited without limit by films or pictures exhibited or sold in places of public accommodation any more than live sex and nudity can be exhibited or sold without limit in such public places. At a minimum, prurient, patently-offensive depiction or description of sexual conduct must have serious literary, artistic, political or scientific value to merit First Amendment protection.

Under the holdings announced today, no one will be subject to prosecution for the same or exposure of obscene materials unless these materials depict or describe patently offensive "hardcore" sexual conduct specifically defined by the regulating state law, as written or construed.

Mr. Justice Brennan also notes, and we agree, that "uncertainty of the standards creates a continuing source of tension between state and federal courts. The problem is that one cannot say with certainty that material is obscene until at least five members of this court, applying inevitably obscure standards, have pronounced it so."

But today, for the first time since Roth was decided in 1957, a majority of this Court has agreed on concrete guidelines to isolate "hard-core" pornography from expression protected by the First Amendment.

This may not be an easy road, freed from difficulty. But no amount of "fatigue" should lead us to adopt a convenient "institutional rationale—an abolutist, anything goes view of the First Amendment—because it will lighten our burdens."

Under a national constitution, fundamental First Amendment limitations on the powers of the states do not vary from community to community, but this does not mean that there are, or should or can be, fixed, uniform national standards of precisely what appeals to the "prurient interest" or "patently offensive."

It is neither realistic nor constitutionally sound to read the First Amendment as requiring that the people of Maine or Mississippi accept public depiction of conduct found tolerable in Las Vegas or New York City.

As the Court made clear in Miskin v. New York, the primary concern with requiring a jury to apply the standard of "the average person, applying contemporary community standards" is to be certain that so far as material is not aimed at a deviant group, it will be judged by its impact on an average person, rather than a particularly susceptible or sensitive person—or indeed a totally insensitive one.

The dissenting Justices sound the alarm of repression. But, in our view, to equate the free and robust exchange of ideas and political debate with commercial exploitation of obscene material demeans the grand conception of the First Amendment and its high purposes in the historic struggle for freedom.

Mr. Justice Brennan finds "it is hard to see how state-ordered regimentation of our minds can ever be forestalled." These doleful anticipations assume that courts cannot distinguish commerce in ideas, protected by the First Amendment, from commercial exploitation of obscene material.

Moreover, state regulation of hard-core pornography so as to make it unavailable to nonadults, a regulation which Mr. Justice Brennan finds constitutionally permissible, has all the elements of "censorship" for adults; indeed even more rigid enforcement techniques may be called for with such dichotomy of regulation.

One can concede that the "sexual revolution" of recent years may have had useful by-products in striking layers of prudery from a subject long irrationally kept from needed ventilation. But it does not follow that no regulation of patently offensive "hard-core" material is needed or permissible; civilized people do not allow unregulated access to heroin because it is a derivative of medicinal morphine.

JOSEPH P. LORDI, PROSECUTOR OF ESSEX COUNTY
Plaintiff, v. UA New Jersey Theatres, Inc.,
A New Jersey Corp., et al.
108 N. J. Super. 19
December 9, 1968

Mintz, J. S. G.

Consolidated proceedings alleging that motion picture film was obscene within purview of statute and seeking to enjoin showing of the film. The Superior Court, Chancery Division, Mintz, J. S. G., held that although the dominant theme of the motion picture, "I Am Curious (Yellow)," taken as a whole, appealed to prurient interest, and although the film was patently offensive because it affronted contemporary community standards relating to the description or representation of sexual matters, the film was not "obscene" where it did possess modicum of social value.

Order in accordance with opinion.

In these consolidated proceedings the prosecutors of Essex, Union and Middlesex Counties allege that the motion picture film entitled, "I Am Curious (Yellow)," is obscene within the purview of N. J. S. A. 2A:115-1.1 et seq. They seek to enjoin the showing of this film in the theatres in their respective counties. N. J. S. A. 2A:115-3.5. The prosecutor of Bergen County did not file a formal complaint but indicated that he would abide by the judgment of the court in these proceedings. Defendants deny that the motion picture is obscene within the meaning of N. J. S. A. 2A:115-1.1 and affirmatively assert that it is within the area of constitutionally-protected freedom of speech and press under the First and Fourteenth Amendments to the Constitution of the United States, and Article I, par. 6 of the Constitution of the State of New Jersey.

"I Am Curious (Yellow)" was produced in Sweden. The dialogue is in Swedish with English subtitles added. This film was adjudged not obscene in a 2-1 decision in United States v. A Motion Picture Film Entitled, "I Am Curious—Yellow," 404 F. 2d 196 (2d Cir. 1968). The court reversed a judgment of forfeiture and confiscation entered in the federal district court upon a jury verdict of obscenity. Judge Hays, writing for the majority, recognized that there may be differences of opinion as to what the picture is "about," but said:

> It would perhaps not be demonstrably wrong to say that it is concerned with that subject which has become such a commonplace in contemporary fiction and drama, the search for identity. It is the story of a young girl who is trying to work out her relationship to such political, social and economic problems as the possibility of a classless society, the acceptance of the Franco regime, and the policy and practice of nonviolence. At one point the girl experiments with oriental religious ritual and meditation. The girl's interpersonal relationships are also pictured, including particularly her relation to her father, presented as an idealist who has become disillusioned and has given up meaningful activity. A fairly large portion of the film is devoted to the relations between the girl and her young lover.
>
> A number of different techniques are employed in the production of the film. For example, much of the early part is in terms of "cinema verite," showing the girl asking questions on subjects of public importance of the ordinary man or woman in the street. The problem of the nature of reality is suggested by passages representing the girl's fantasies and by the injection into story of material concerning the making of the picture itself, such as the director's relations with the

leading actress. There are a number of scenes which show the young girl and her lover nude. Several scenes depict sexual intercourse under varying circumstances, some of them quite unusual. There are scenes of oral-genital activity. [at 198].

The sex scenes leave very little to the imagination. One unusual scene is an episode of copulation in the crook of a very large old tree. Nearby a group of fundamentalist Christians are singing. There was testimony to the effect that this scene symbolizes the rebellion of youth against authority and tradition. There is also a scene of intercourse on the balustrade of the Royal Palace in Stockholm, in rhythm to the Swedish National Anthem while a palace guard endeavors to stand at attention watching the antics of the lovers. Apparently this was intended as a humorous incident and was explained by some witnesses as symbolic of the rebellion of youth against authority. Other sexual scenes are shown with greater candor.

The sexual content is frankly presented and, as Judge Hays observed in "I Am Curious—Yellow," supra, "with greater explicitness than has been seen in any other film produced for general viewing. The question for decision is whether, going farther in this direction than any previous production, the film exceeds the limits established by the courts." [at 198].

N. J. S. A. 2A:115-1.1 provides that:

(a) The word "obscene" wherever it appears in the chapter to which this act is a supplement shall mean that which to the average person, applying contemporary community standards, when considered as a whole, has as its dominant theme or purpose an appeal to prurient interest.

(b) Any book, publication, picture, writing, record or other mechanical or electronic audio or visual reproduction or other material shall be obscene within the meaning of subsection (a) hereof if it is established that:

(1) The dominant theme of the material taken as a whole appeals to a prurient interest;
(2) The material is patently offensive because it affronts contemporary community standards relating to the description or representation of sexual matters; and
(3) The material is utterly without redeeming social value.

This statute is a codification of the law finally enunciated in Mr. Justice Brennan's opinion for the United States Supreme Court in A Book Named "John Cleland's Memoirs of a Woman of Pleasure" v. Massachusetts, 383 U. S. 413, 86 S. Ct. 975, 16 L. Ed. 2d 1 (1966), hereinafter referred to as Memoirs. As observed in that opinion, all three criteria set forth in the cited statute must coalesce to justify a finding of obscenity. Each of the three criteria is to be applied independently. The social value of the film can neither be weighed against nor canceled by its prurient appeal or patent offensiveness. If the material in question possesses only a modicum of social value, it is not "utterly without redeeming social value." Memoirs, at 419, 86 S. Ct. 975.

(1, 2) All ideas having even the slightest redeeming social importance—unorthodox ideas, controversial ideas, even ideas hateful to the prevailing climate of opinion—have the protection of the First Amendment unless excludable because they encroach upon the limited area of more important interests. The protection given speech and press was fashioned to assure unfettered interchange of ideas for the bringing about of political and social changes desired by the people. However, obscenity is not within the area of constitutionally protected speech or press. Roth v. United States, 354 U. S. 476, 484, 77 S. Ct. 1304, 1 L. Ed. 2d 1498 (1957). But cf. Stanley v. Georgia, 394 U. S. 557, 89 S. Ct. 1243, 22 L. Ed. 2d 542 (1969).

Judge Hays stated in "I Am Curious—Yellow," supra, that the nudity and sexual activity depicted is part of an artistic whole and is united with and related to the story and the characters which are presented. He held that although sexual conduct may be one of its principal themes:

> It cannot be said that "the dominant theme of the material taken as a whole appeals to a prurient interest in sex." Whatever the dominant theme may be said to be *** it is certainly not sex. Moreover, not only is the sexual theme subordinate, but it is handled in such a way as to make it at least extremely doubtful that interest in it should be characterized as "prurient."
>
> It is even more clear that "I Am Curious" is not utterly without redeeming social value. *** [I]t is quite certain that "I Am Curious" does present ideas and does strive to present these ideas artistically. It falls within the ambit of intellectual effort that the first amendment was designed to protect. [404 F. 2d at 199-200].

Judge Friendly, in a separate concurring opinion, stated that Judge Hays' opinion demonstrates the required modicum of social value in the film. He relied solely upon this fact in finding it not obscene and concluded:

> I would agree that the presence of 'redeeming social value' should not save the day if the sexual episodes were simply lugged in and bore no relationship whatever to the theme, a truly pornographic film would not be rescued by inclusion of a few verses from the Psalms. While this case may come somewhat close to the line, I cannot conscientiously

say that a connection between the serious purpose and the sexual episodes and displays of nudity is wholly wanting. [at 201].

Chief Judge Lumbard filed a dissenting opinion in which he stated:

Whatever one can say about the alleged significance of the film, which to this captive onlooker was a continuous and unrelieved boredom except for the sexual scenes, it is almost impossible to remember anything about it. The only impact the picture has and the only impact it was designed to have are the sexual scenes; its only interest to the viewer arises from the uncertainty of the method of mutual sexual gratification in which hero and heroine will next indulge.

While the sex is heterosexual, the participants indulge in acts of fellatio and cunnilingus. Needless to say these acts bear no conceivable relevance to any social value, except that of box-office appeal. Moreover, the sexual scenes have nothing whatever to do with the remainder of the picture. Obviously the only interest aroused for the average person is a prurient interest. Nor is it persuasive that the explicit sex scenes take only about ten minutes out of 120. The enormous visual impact of a motion picture as distinguished from other media cannot be disregarded. Cf. Freedman v. Maryland, 380 U. S. 51, 61, 85 S. Ct. 734, 13 L. Ed. 2d 649 (1965). The combination of sight and sound, in the darkness of the movie theatre, result in a uniquely forceful impact on the audience. Because of the nature of this medium, sexual scenes in a motion picture may transcend the bounds of constitutional protection long before a frank description of the same scenes in a book or magazine. Cf. Landau v. Fording, 245 Cal. App. 2d 820, 54 Cal. Rptr. 177 (1966), aff'd per curiam, 388 U. S. 456, 87 S. Ct. 2109, 18 L. Ed. 2d 1317 (1967). *** [at 203].

The film in question has also been the subject of litigation in several other jurisdictions, with conflicting results. This court viewed the film and is called upon to make an independent judgment, giving such consideration as it deems appropriate to the expert testimony presented before it. Whether or not the motion picture should be suppressed requires ascertainment of the "dim and uncertain line" that often separates obscenity from constitutionally-protected expression. Bantam Books v. Sullivan, 372 U. S. 58, 66, 83 S. Ct. 631, 9 L. Ed. 2d 584 (1963).

(4) My conclusion is that the dominant theme of this motion picture taken as a whole appeals to a prurient interest. I also find that the film is patently offensive because it affronts contemporary community standards relating to the description or representation of sexual matters. The crucial issue is whether the motion picture is utterly without redeeming social value. There was considerable testimony presented on this criterion by plaintiffs and defendants.

The defense also offered into evidence a series of reviews by film critics which were received for the limited purpose of showing that the film was seriously treated in respected publications as follows: Vincent Canby in the New York Times, John Simon, in the New York Times, Richard Schickel in Life, Leonard Gross in Look, William Wolf in Cue, Hollis

Alpert in Saturday Review, Richard Atcheson in Holiday, Liz Smith in Cosmopolitan, Stanley Kauffmann in The New Republic, Leroy F. Aarons in The Washington Post, Ted Mahar in The Portland Oregonian, Bernard L. Drew in The Hartford Times and Stephen Allen in The Camden Courier-Post.

Plaintiffs offered into evidence the reviews of Alan Adelson in the Wall Street Journal, Rex Reed in the New York Times, Nancy Razen in the Newark Star Ledger, Charles Champlin in the Los Angeles Times, and James Kilpatrick in the Los Angeles Times.

While I do not unqualifiedly accept everything the experts for the defense had to say on whether or not the film is utterly without redeeming social value, I believe that their collective testimony was clearly more persuasive than that of plaintiffs and amply reflects the required "modicum of social value." Memoirs, supra. And I concur in Judge Friendly's finding to which I made earlier reference and state, as he did, that I cannot conscientiously find that a connection between the serious purpose of the film and the sexual episodes and displays of the nudity is wholly lacking.

However, plaintiffs urge that the alleged pandering of the movie should be decisive in finding that it is utterly without redeeming social value. They argue that the film has been advertised in a manner calculated to capitalize on its extensive portrayals of nudity and sexual activity, rather than its supposed serious message, and thus falls within the condemnation of Ginzburg v. United States, supra. The court there said that "* * * Where the purveyor's sole emphasis is on the sexually-provocative aspects of his publications, that fact may be decisive in the determination of obscenity." (383 U. S., at 470, 86 S. Ct., at 947, emphasis added.) The pandering doctrine established in Ginzburg has been substantially incorporated in our statutory law. N. J. S. A. 2A:115-1.2 provides that:

In any prosecution under the provisions of the chapter to which this act is a supplement, evidence of pandering or evidence that the sale or distribution of the material in question was exploited on the basis of its appeal to prurient interest, may be considered in determining whether the material is utterly without redeeming social value.

Plaintiff's charge of pandering is based solely upon the sale and distribution of the scenario of the film which is contained in a paperback book sold to the general public. The scenario was designed to generate an interest in the motion picture. It is argued that this scenario contains a disproportionately high percentage of pictures of sexual activities and nudity in comparison to the number of such scenes in the film. Hence, it is asserted that pandering operates to negate whatever redeeming social value the film might otherwise have and renders it obscene. In Ginzburg, supra, the Court did not deal with a civil action for the suppression of a book or movie, as we are here concerned with, but rather with a criminal action based on the alleged distribution of obscene literature through the mails. While Mr. Justice Brennan's opinion for the court indicated that pandering properly could be a decisive factor in a determination of obscenity, he also emphasized that criminal convictions of defendants did not necessarily imply suppression of the materials involved, nor chill their proper distribution for a proper use. 383 U. S., at 470, 471, 475, 86 S. Ct. 942.

In the present civil actions plaintiffs seek to enjoin the showing of the film in question. Ginzburg and the instant cases are factually distinguishable. In Ginzburg there was abundant evidence to sustain the finding that the sole emphasis in the advertising was on the sexually provocative aspects of the publications. In the case at bar the newspaper advertising has been completely devoid of any such appeal. There is no claim that the advertising of the film at the theatres here involved is objectionable. The title "I Am Curious (Yellow)" is not suggestive of any appeal to prurient interests. The cover on the paperback book is equally innocuous. Additionally, the book contains not only the scenario of the film, but also excerpts from the testimony of expert witnesses in the United States District Court proceeding to which I have earlier alluded. Both have some redeeming social value and advertise the movie, at least in part, on the basis of its political and social themes. The book which now sells for $1.75 was at the time of this trial available in Newark bookstores, approximately twelve miles from the Colony Theatre in Livingston where the film is currently being shown. There was no testimony respecting the availability of the book in Middlesex or Union Counties. Under all the stated circumstances, I cannot find that the advertising of the film unduly emphasizes its sexually provocative aspects.

It is plaintiffs' burden to prove that the film is utterly without redeeming social value. They have failed to do so. On the basis of all the evidence I reluctantly and with regret conclude that "I Am Curious (Yellow)" does possess a modicum of redeeming social value.

STUDENT PERSONNEL ADMINISTRATORS AND RECOMMENDATIONS FOR CONTRACTED OUTSIDE SERVICES

Given the financial stringency of many public and private institutions, student personnel administrators, in particular, should examine those service areas which most readily lend themselves to contracted outside services. Such services may include food, books and supplies, health, residence and maintenance. Professional expertise, in addition to university savings, can often be secured by using commercial contracted services. The student personnel administrator, however, must be able to accurately assess not only the appropriateness of securing such outside services, but he also must help make the best possible contract. This involves knowing campus service needs and the best means to satisfy those needs.

The student personnel administrator should seek legal guidance in making contractual relationships, and be aware of the following areas of significance:

1. *Credit Ratings*

It is wise to secure a credit rating for those with whom a long-term contract or contract involving substantial sums of money is contemplated. A bankruptcy with its concomitant discharge of creditors or adverse litigation can unnecessarily complicate and even frustrate the fundamental purpose of utilizing contracted outside services.

2. *Past Performance*

Prior clients should be polled as to their satisfaction with the proposed outside contractor. Fees previously charged also should be examined so that costs can be controlled. At least three prior clients should be questioned.

3. *Time Period*

Annual contracts with termination clauses of at least ninety days prior notice are generally desirable. Most contracts should be limited to one year so that greater control of the quality of services can be maintained. In addition, costs can then be projected on an annual basis to the benefit of contractor and contractee.

4. *Insurance*

The parameters of tort liability and workmen's compensation insurance should be delineated. Separate areas of responsibility for each contracting party should be clearly identified. Premiums for insurance costs are generally the responsibility of the outside contractor. Hold harmless agreements, if any, should be carefully scrutinized. All cancellation provisions by the insurance company or the insured should have at least a thirty-day prior notice clause.

5. *Equal Opportunity*

The student personnel administrator, notwithstanding legal requirement precluding discrimination in the hiring or assigning of personnel, should include a provision to this effect in the contract itself.

6. *Permits and Licenses*

The outside contractor should assume at his own expense all necessary federal, state or municipal licenses for the operation of his business. The outside contractor also should assume the responsibility for the payment of any governmental taxes which may be assessed against its property or business while in or upon the University's premises.

7. *Conflict of Laws*

The student personnel administrator should ensure in his contract that in the event of a breach, the law to be utilized will be the law of the state in which the university is situated.

UNIVERSITY LIABILITY FOR THE
ACTIVITIES OF STUDENT ORGANIZATIONS

College and university counsel have traditionally maintained that student activities fees charged and collected by a university are the property of that university. A university, therefore, is obligated to insure that such fees are used for lawful purposes. The use of student fees in behalf of political candidates or political organizations, moreover, may well jeopardize the exempt status of a university under relevant provisions of the Internal Revenue Code.

Universities generally accord to student governing bodies substantial discretion in terms of the expenditure of student activities monies. Indeed, such monies are allocated to campus organizations for a variety of purposes including the printing and publication of newspapers and magazines. University administrators should understand that in point of law, institutional responsibility for fee-funded campus organizations remains intact, not withstanding the autonomy of student governing groups. Institutional disclaimers of liability stating that the opinions expressed in student publications are not those of the university are generally ineffective and have no legal significance.

As an illustration of university responsibility, the publication in student newspapers of advertisements concerning potentially illegal services or products may be considered. Counseling and referral services with respect to securing abortions is one example. Although the newspapers in which such advertisements appear are under the direction of student editors and published primarily for a student readership because costs for publication are paid from university-collected monies, the university, in point of law, is the publisher and liable for violation of relevant civil and criminal statutes.

University liability for the activities of student organizations may be diminished and even eliminated when such organizations are independently incorporated and sustained by funds solicited and collected by the organizations themselves.

STUDENT PERSONNEL ADMINISTRATORS AND GUIDELINES FOR THEIR CAMPUS AND CIVIC RELATIONSHIPS

Deans of students can play an important role in the campus community, and help provide the educational cement which brings together the various university constituencies. Recommendations for creating a sense of cooperative interaction among the various individuals and groups within and around the academic community follow:

1. Chief Executive—The dean of students or vice president for student affairs should report directly to the chief executive. The dean, as an equal member of the campus or university administration, should help evaluate academic and student service programs as they affect the intellectual and personal development of the student. The chief executive should expect from his dean a sophisticated analysis of student educational trends, both in terms of personal lifestyle and academic orientation. The dean should assume full responsibility for all services under his authority.

2. Faculty—The dean of students should encourage the faculty to seek his advice with students in personal or academic difficulty. Conversely, i.e. the dean should seek advice from faculty. The dean should involve faculty members in orientation programs, student governance and student activities. Committees on student life and student services should be structured so as to include interested faculty members.

3. Students—The dean of students should think of himself as a teacher. The dean, in working with students and staff, should be able to articulate meaningful alternatives to problem situations. The dean's primary role should be that of teacher-counselor. This role should not necessarily restrict the dean's obligation to stay student behavior which is damaging to other students or the institution itself. The dean should actively encourage face-to-face relationships by students with faculty, staff, alumni and people of the community.

5. Media—The dean has the obligation to meet with members of the press, radio and TV so that objective and rational assessments of student life can be made. The dean should not make casual judgments about student behavior, and his comments to the media should be based on carefully-studied data. Inflammatory remarks

regarding students or any member of the community should be avoided.

6. Parents—The dean should not assume the vote of surrogate parent. He should be available, however, so that parents can meet with him regarding their son or daughter's personal and academic progress.

7. Criminal Justice—The dean should recognize that he is neither policeman, prosecutor nor judge. As an educator, the dean should restrict his involvement to those areas which legitimately require his participation. The dean should not attempt, furthermore, to impose his own opinions regarding a student's guilt or innocence upon the Courts. In addition, the dean should not allow the Courts to arrogate his role as educator.

Index

A

Administrator, student personnel, 3-4, private, 57; public, 57
Alcoholic beverages, 92

B

Bogust, et al. v. Iverson, 17
Brown v. The Board of Education, 110

C

Collective bargaining, 118
Comprehensive Drug Abuse Prevention and Control Act of 1970, 6, 9
Confidentiality, 58; of records, 83
Contract, enrollment, 29, 33; residence, 30; outside services, 134
Contract theory, 8, 13
Controlled dangerous substances, 55, 68
Courts, role of, 5, 110

D

Dean of students, 6, 33, 112-113, 137
De communitatis, 8-9
Democratized colleague approach, 4
Discipline, 31, 33; memorandum on judicial standards, 43
Dissent, guidelines for, 94
Domicile, 30
Drugs, 55, user of, 65, narcotic, 69
Due process clause, 6, 31

E

Education, definition of, 5
Enrollment contract, 29, 33
Esteban v. Central Missouri State College, 23
Evidence, 57

F

Fiduciary theory, 8, 17
Fifth Amendment, 6, 31
Financial aid, 31
First Amendment, 82-83, 99, 104, 106
Fourteenth Amendment, 6, 31, 43, 48, 57
Fourth Amendment, 56-57
Freedom of association, 83, 106
Freedom of speech, 82

G

Gott v. Berea College, et al., 9

H

Hammond v. South Carolina State College, 99
Healy, et al., Petitioners v. James, et al., 106

I

Inherent power theory, 23
In loco parentis, 4, 7, 9, 56
In re Gault, 56
Insurance, 31, 117

J

Jones v. Vassar College, 13
Judicial systems, with regard to campus disciplinary proceedings, 33; flow chart, 95, 97

K

Knight v. State Board of Education, 37

L

Law, definition of, 3, 4
Legal counsel, 3